Guide For Reducing Quality Costs

Second Edition

Quality Costs Committee
Jack Campenella
Chairman, Quality Costs Committee

AMERICAN SOCIETY FOR QUALITY CONTROL
310 West Wisconsin Avenue
Milwaukee, Wisconsin 53203

Guide for Reducing Quality Costs
Quality Costs Committee

Published by the American Society for Quality Control, Milwaukee, Wisconsin.

2nd edition, 1987
1st edition, 1980

ISBN 0-87389-029-9

MEMBERS OF THE TASK GROUP
ON GUIDE FOR REDUCING QUALITY COSTS

W. N. Moore — Westinghouse Electric Corporation
Task Group Chairman

Andrew F. Grimm — C&F Stamping Company

Clay Brewer — General Electric Company

Edgar W. Dawes — Digital Equipment Corporation

Richard K. Dobbins — Honeywell, Inc.

John T. Hagan — Consultant

John R. Lavery — Diebold, Inc.

R.C. Rhodes — Consultant

William O. Winchell — General Motors Corporation

TABLE OF CONTENTS

GUIDE FOR REDUCING QUALITY COSTS

PURPOSE

The purpose of this document is to provide guidance to general management and professionals engaged in quality program management to enable them to structure and manage programs for quality costs reduction.

A more detailed discussion of quality costs may be found in the ASQC publications, *Principles of Quality Costs*, and *Guide for Managing Supplier Quality Costs*. *Guide for Reducing Quality Costs* describes techniques for using those costs in programs to reduce costs and, thereby, improve profits.

In using this guide, it must be understood that improving conformance quality results in lower total quality costs. Total quality costs include elements incurred in marketing, design, purchasing, manufacture and service. In short, every part of the product cycle typically generates some quality costs, and programs for identifying and improving cost must be comprehensive enough to involve all these functions.

The following sections of this guide discuss the philosophy of quality improvement, use of quality costs, techniques for reducing failure and appraisal costs, and methods for prevention of excessive quality costs. Several case histories are contained in section on "Examples".

WHAT IS QUALITY?

This guide uses the word "quality" quite differently than it is often used in industry. More often than not quality now means conformance to drawings and specifications and quality control determines if the product conforms. In this guide, quality is used in a broader sense and means fitness for customer use. When quality is defined this way, it encompasses both quality of design and quality of conformance, and programs for quality improvement must encompass all phases of product life, from design through use by the customer. The quality costs programs described in this manual are designed to identify and help solve quality problems in all phases of product life. All uses of the word quality in this manual will be in this context.

THE QUALITY COST IMPROVEMENT PHILOSOPHY

It is a fact, too often not recognized, that every dollar saved in the total cost of quality is directly translatable into a dollar of pre-tax earnings. It is also a fact that quality improvements and quality cost reductions cannot be legislated by management demand — they have to be earned by the hard process of problem-solving. The first step in the process is the identification of problems; a problem in this context is defined as an area of high quality costs. Every problem identified by quality costs is an opportunity for profit improvement.

This guide is about a quality program that is *not* confined to the control of quality in the manufacturing stage. Most people recognize that product quality is determined by many factors outside this stage, but many quality programs do not concern themselves with these factors. In some cases, quality program efforts have been attempts at not allowing things to get any worse (control) instead of striving to make things better (improvement). As a result, things have gotten worse in many places simply because controls are not — and never can be 100% effective. Improving quality is much like improving product costs. It is everybody's job and everybody is for the idea, but, until there is management commitment to improve and a formal program for forcing improvement, it just doesn't happen.

This guide describes what each company function must do to satisfy the customer's needs and reduce quality costs. Also described are ways to prevent the production of defects through involvement of people in marketing, design, purchasing, accounting, manufacturing, and quality assurance. It describes ways to find problems and correct their causes. It tells you how to use the costs associated with quality and how to reduce those costs.

Quality improvement results in cost improvement. Designing and building a product right the first time always costs less. With existing products, solving problems by finding their causes and eliminating them results in measurable savings. To cash in on these savings the quality performance of the past must be improved, and this guide describes ways to do that.

Figure 1 shows how quality costs analysis bridges the gap between the elements of a prevention-oriented quality program and the means used by general management to measure performance — the profit and loss statement.

This chart shows the flow of quality costs information from the working quality assurance level to the total cost of quality level and ultimately to the profit and loss statement. Every dollar saved because of improved quality has a direct impact on profit!

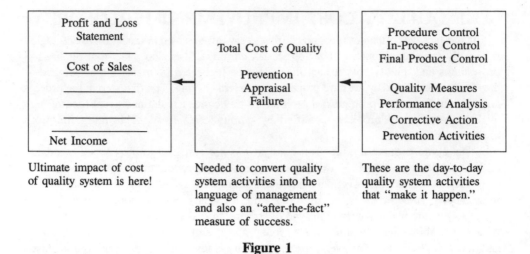

Figure 1
Quality Cost System

USEFULNESS OF QUALITY COSTS

Quality costs are useful for strategic planning and programming quality improvement.

STRATEGIC PLANNING

Strategic quality program planning is vital to the continuing profitability of many segments of American industry. The pressures for safer, cleaner, and more reliable products are becoming stronger each year. We must find ways to meet these increasing demands and still remain competitive. The key to achieving this is to improve quality using the methods described in this guide and reduce costs as a result.

To improve quality and reduce quality costs, there has to be a trigger for making changes in the status quo. The firm's strategic plan is an ideal device to force changes and the inclusion of quality and quality costs improvement plans in the overall strategic plan is recommended. This gives the quality and quality costs situation the management visibility that is to often lacking. When quality and quality costs improvements are set forth as business objectives (along with the more conventional business objectives) against which management performance is evaluated, there is effective motivation for action.

Today's quality program must be directed toward improved product quality and reduced quality costs. The quality manager must develop strategic quality plans that will assure continuous quality improvement. This program must be integrated into total company planning activities. Strategic quality planning is a continuous process of evaluations, decisions, and actions. All activities, customer demands, competitor's activities, the history of the quality role, and the future quality role must be considered in this planning.

Strategic quality planning should become a key ingredient in total planning because of the planning concepts it signifies — completeness, advantageous position, thoroughness, cleverness, skillfulness, integrated action, and economic orientation. A strategy is a plan of action for allocating resources to achieve an objective. Strategic planning involves analysis to determine a strategy and actions to implement the strategy. Some of the advantages of strategic quality planning activities are that they:

- Will reduce planning time once it has been started because it is a continuous cycle.
- Are realistic because they consider all variables.
- Will result in a stronger quality program because they force involvement by other departments.
- Will improve quality decisions because of the forced evaluation of many alternatives.

Relationship Between Quality Costs and Strategic Planning

Quality costs for a profit center are made up of costs incurred in several activities. Figure 2 shows the buildup of costs from all functional departments into an overall quality costs analysis for the entire profit center.

As can be seen, quality costs are incurred by all major functions in an organization, so problem areas can exist anywhere. Careful analysis must be done to find the most costly problems and programs must be developed to attack them. Many times a strategic program is needed. When this need exists, a strategic quality program should be developed using inputs from all functions and it should become a part of the profit center's overall strategic program. Figure 3 shows the relationship between the overall strategic program and the quality program.

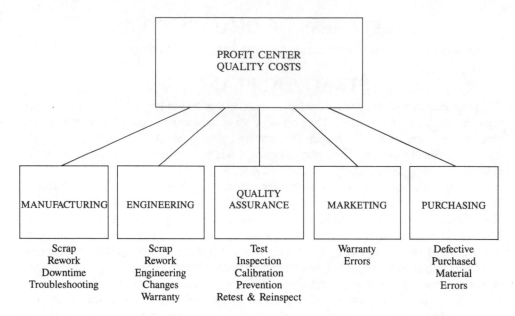

Figure 2

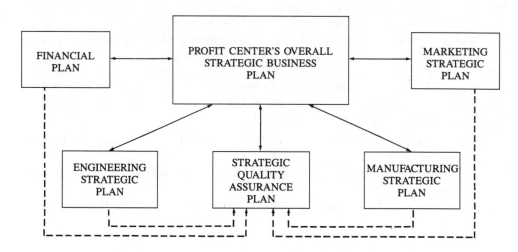

Figure 3

The Planning Process

Strategic planning should be done by a step-by-step process. The basic steps include:

- Reviewing past performance and present position
- Appraising the environment
- Setting objectives
- Selecting a strategy
- Implementing the strategic program
- Reporting and evaluating the plan

The final step in the cycle provides needed input for the first step so that planning becomes a continuous process. Following are general considerations for accomplishing each step in the cycle.

Review Past Performance and Present Position

A thorough review provides a realistic assessment of past performance, current conditions, and future potential. Typical indicators of the actual situation that should be reviewed are customer complaints, quality costs, reject rates, scrap rates, and test results. One good tool for accomplishing the review is the quality audit, which will point out weaknesses in quality, manufacturing, product design, or other aspects of the overall quality program. Four fundamental questions that should be asked during the review are:

- What kind of quality program do we have?
- Why *this* quality program?
- What explains success or lack of it?
- What changes are taking place?

Attempting to truthfully answer these questions will raise other revealing questions, point out performance against past objectives, and provide the necessary framework for effective planning.

The degree of research that goes into the review will vary with each situation, but it is critical that the review be undertaken. You have to know where you have been and where you are now in order to decide where you should be in the future.

Appraise the Environment

There are numerous environmental factors that may interact significantly with the quality programs. Typical examples are:

- The activities of other departments.
- Changes in customer demands.
- New safety and liability regulations.
- Actions of competitors.

These environmental factors are of three types:

- Factors that are fixed and that quality management can do little about (e.g. existing contracts, liability laws and judgments, safety regulations, military standards).
- Factors that quality management can partially influence (e.g., product designs, methods, equipments, industry standards, society regulations).
- Factors that quality management can control to a considerable degree (e.g., quality standards, inspection and test plans, drawing and specification control, calibration controls, statistical analysis, new contract content).

By distinguishing the controllable factors from the uncontrollable factors, evaluating the potential implications of each, and continually monitoring the environment, the quality planning function can better understand and include these effects in the total planning program.

Set Objectives

From the knowledge and understanding achieved in the status review and the environmental information, the strengths and weaknesses of the quality program can be identified, and specific objectives with target completion dates can be established. The objectives should include a means of maintaining the strengths and improving the weak areas. Typical quality objectives relate to:

- Defect levels of suppliers.
- Yield rates for processes.
- Quality levels for products.
- Budget planning.
- Quality costs.
- Quality levels for customers.
- Quality influence in company.
- Upgrading quality of personnel.

Attention should be given to identifying both short- and long-range objectives, including priorities for action. The objectives should be frequently reviewed so they can be altered if environmental or other factors change.

Select a Strategy

Once clear objectives have been established, a definite strategy should be formulated and clearly stated.

Consider all possible ways of accomplishing the objectives and develop a group of alternative strategies. Use:

1. Pertinent company information, such as records and reports,
2. Other company strategies,
3. Experience and expertise in the field,
4. Strategic planning of other departments.

Evaluate all the alternatives that appear to have practical application. Consider the:

1. Strengths and weaknesses of the quality program determined from this review,
2. Effect on other departments,
3. Effect of possible customer or competitor changes,
4. Reality of the situation.

Select the final strategy and prepare the strategy statement. Review the:

1. Consistency with other company strategies,
2. Communicable aspects of the strategy,
3. Weakest element of the strategy,
4. Most difficult part to implement,
5. Most significant aspects of the strategy that differ from previous efforts,
6. Economics of the strategy.

Thorough consideration of the steps for selecting a strategy will maximize the probability of attaining the goals.

Implement the Strategic Program

Planning for the implementation of the strategy is the most important step of the planning process. All prior effort leads up to the implementation or action step. There are many cases of "that was a sound strategy, but nothing happened as a result." This situation is due to a failure to follow-up the strategy with appropriate action programs. Key factors in effective action programs are:

- Assignment of project action teams that make best utilization of the available manpower abilities.
- Awareness of team members of the importance of the project, their responsibility and commitment, and management's support of the project.
- Clear definition and description of the project, including publishing of schedules, responsibilities, and milestones.
- Reviews to show the project is still on schedule or that modification or changes are necessary.
- Flexibility in the project to maintain direction toward the established objective.
- Reporting and feedback of the actions and results of the program.

Continuous measurement of the overall action program is essential to maintaining its effectiveness and sustaining it as a long-range management tool.

Report and Evaluate the Plan

The final step in the planning cycle is one of integrating the strategic quality plan into the total strategic plan and evaluating the costs and benefits of the plan. The reporting of the plan should include three documented features.

1. **Summary report of all strategies, including:**
   a. List of all strategies and due dates,
   b. Descriptive statement of each strategy,
   c. Benefits of each strategy,
   d. Costs of each strategy, and
   e. Approval signatures.
2. **Individual report of each strategy, including:**
   a. Name of strategy,
   b. Statement of purpose and objectives,
   c. Description of features — action projects,
   d. Justification — need or cost improvement,
   e. Resources to accomplish — total cost,
   f. Schedule — due dates, and
   g. Adjustments to the plans.
3. **Regular status report of all strategies, including:**
   a. Action to date on all projects,
   b. Costs and benefits to date, and
   c. Adjustments to the plans.

Analysis and measurement of the effectiveness of the program will provide guidance in managing the present program and direction in future strategic planning. By taking the well ordered step-by-step approach to strategic planning the probabilities of accomplishing objectives will be maximized.

Through better planning, quality performance can be improved. Continued achievement of good performance can identify the quality program as a key contributor to the success and assure that quality will play an enlarged role in future plans and activities.

PROGRAMMING IMPROVEMENT

The strategic quality plan describes a management commitment to quality and quality costs improvement. The quality costs data indicate the areas that are candidates for improvement. When the highest cost areas are analyzed in greater detail, many improvement projects become apparent. For example, high warranty costs are a trigger to rank customer failure problems for detailed investigation, with the aim of looking into product design, process control, or inspection planning for the cures to the highest cost problems. Regardless of what the high quality costs category may be, the mere act of identifying it should lead to actions to reduce it.

It is of major importance for management to understand that there are no general solutions to quality problems (i.e., high quality costs areas). These problems are not solved by organizational manipulation, "new" management techniques, not even by quality costs analysis. The quality costs information simply points out problem (opportunity) areas. Once the problem/opportunity area is identified, the detailed nature of the problem has to be investigated and appropriate actions taken. *The entire process of quality improvement and quality cost reduction necessarily is pursued on a problem-by-problem basis.*

Because of high external failure costs, a natural temptation might be to put more emphasis on appraisal efforts, but this approach may simply convert some external failures to internal failures (i.e., scrap, rework) and bear an increased inspection burden.

Similarly, it may be tempting to increase product engineering efforts in a generalized attempt to prevent defects, but a generalized effort may not be very effective. Usually, the improvements are obtained by actions in the prevention category. Effective prevention actions are those aimed at very specific problems — problems that can be spotlighted by the quality costs studies.

To put it succinctly, the process of quality and quality costs improvement depends on understanding cause-and-effect relationships, and the study of total quality costs is probably the most effective tool available to management to obtain this understanding.

In summary, to effectively establish quality improvement efforts, it is necessary to:

- Recognize and organize quality related costs to gain knowledge of magnitude, contributing elements and trends.
- Analyze quality performance, identify major problem areas, and measure product line and/or manufacturing section performance.
- Implement effective corrective action and cost improvement programs.
- Evaluate effect of action to assure intended results.
- Program activities for maximum dollar pay off and maximum effective manpower utilization.
- Budget quality work to meet objectives.

THE QUALITY SYSTEM

Perhaps the most important result of the collection, analysis, and use of quality costs is the exposure given to the total quality system as it really exists in the organization. The collection of costs forces definition of all activities contributing to the quality of the product. Analysis of quality costs data forces evaluation of the effectiveness of the contribution of each activity, the relationships among the many activities, and the all-important communications links that tie activities together.

Each organization will define its quality system differently, but the overriding requirement is that whatever definition is used must be comprehensive. That is, *it must include all efforts that affect product quality,* wherever the efforts are accomplished in the organization.

The quality system must involve more than inspection and test in the manufacturing phase. Every department has a responsibility for assuring that the customer's quality requirements are met. The responsibilities for quality must be clearly assigned. Quality is everyone's responsibility, but unless every department fully understands what is expected, quality is likely to suffer. Each person is apt to assume that someone else is taking care of the problems. The responsibilities for quality assigned to each department vary from company to company. They depend on a number of factors, such as differences in organization, the type of product, and the nature of the customer's quality requirements. Most frequently, however, the responsibilities are assigned in the following way:

Marketing
- Liaison with customer.
- Determine the customer's quality requirements and acceptable quality levels.
- Assure that the product quality requirements and any quality system requirements are defined clearly and completely.
- Investigate the customer's opinion of the product quality and performance.
- Continually report this opinion to the department concerned.

Engineering
- Design quality and safety into the product.
- Design products that comply with the customer's quality requirements.
- Prepare specifications that accurately define these requirements.

Manufacturing
- Challenge any drawings or specifications that would be too expensive or impractical to meet.
- Provide facilities capable of meeting the quality requirements.
- Manufacture and deliver products that comply with the drawings and specifications developed by engineering.

Quality Assurance
- Assure that the product meets the customer's quality requirements.
- Establish economical controls for preventing defective products.
- Assure that specific quality costs objectives are established and achieved.

Purchasing
- Select suppliers who are capable of complying with our quality requirements.
- Keep suppliers informed of current quality requirements.
- Work with suppliers to correct quality problems.

Controller
- Keep management informed about the costs of quality.
- Provide cost breakdowns so that problem areas can be identified and corrective action justified.
- Provide accurate data on costs generated by in-plant operations and on those generated by returned material and product warranties.

Industrial Relations
- Recognize the impact of the human factor on quality.
- Develop and implement recruiting, selection, placement, training and upgrading procedures that will result in a work force capable of meeting customer quality requirements.
- Communicate regularly to employees on the need for, and the importance of, working to quality standards.

If there is a weakness in the quality system, it is usually a deficiency in the integration of the elements and their sub-elements into a working whole. Almost every manager can look at his system elements and convince himself that his organization has something going in each area. Perhaps he even has a shelf full of procedures manuals to prove it. However, much of what is actually going on in the quality system might be superficial or might not be well integrated into the operations and traditions of the total organization.

The concept of quality costs is a potent tool for management precisely because it can be used to force the integration of all the separate quality activities into the mainstream of the product cycle; that is, into a total quality system. It forces the entire organization to examine each cost element (and each quality related activity) in the context of the total quality cost (and total quality system).

FINDING THE PROBLEM AREAS

When quality costs are displayed to managers who have not been exposed to the concept, the initial question is likely to be "how much should they be?" or "how does this compare with other organizations or products?" Unfortunately, it is not practical to establish any meaningful absolute standards for such cost comparisons. A quality costs system should be "tailored" to a particular company's needs, so as to perceive trends of significance and furnish objective evidence for management decisions as to where assurance efforts should be placed for optimum return. The search for industry guidelines or other standards of comparison, while natural, is quite dangerous, since it leads to quality costs emphasis for "score-carding" instead of utilization as a management tool for improving the status quo.

The futility of establishing meaningful absolute quality costs guidelines is more apparent if you consider:

1. Inherent key variations in how companies interpret and capture quality costs data;
2. Critical differences in product complexity, process methods and stability, production volume, market characteristics, management needs and objectives, customer reactions, etc.; and,
3. The awkwardness or inappropriateness for many companies of the most prevalent form of quality costs measure (% of net sales billed), considering effect of time differences between time of sales billing and incurrence of actual quality costs.

This last factor is particularly important for periods involving an expanding or contracting product volume or mix, unstable market pricing, shifting sales/leasing revenue ratios, or changing competitive performance criteria. Accordingly, it is much more productive to abandon efforts to compare your quality costs measurements with other companies in favor of meaningful analysis of the problem areas contributing most significantly to *your* quality costs, so that suitable corrective actions can be initiated.

Analysis techniques for qualtiy costs are as varied as those used for any other quality problems in industry. They range from simple charting techniques to complicated mathematical models of the program. In this section of the guide, several of the most common techniques will be discussed and examples of their use will be given. The most common techniques are: trend analysis and Pareto analysis, by element group, department, product, or other groupings.

Trend Analysis

Trend analysis is simply comparing present cost levels to past levels. It is suggested that costs be collected for *at least* one year before attempting to draw conclusions or plan action programs. The data from this one year (minimum) period should be plotted in several ways. Costs associated with each element grouping (prevention, appraisal, internal failure and external failure) should be plotted by month as both total dollars and as a fraction of several measurement bases thought to be appropriate for future use as indicators of business activity. Elements contributing a high proportion of the costs within a grouping should be plotted and analyzed separately. In Figure 4 are plots of total costs in a hypothetical company with costs expressed as dollars per unit produced and as a percentage of gross sales billed.

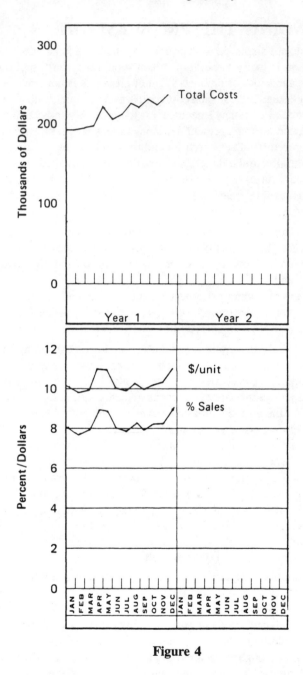

Figure 4

The graphs show that total costs are increasing but that total costs as related to units produced and sales are not changing significantly. Figures 5 & 6 are graphs showing element groups as total dollars and related to the same two bases.

Quality Costs — Total Dollars
(00-s Omitted)

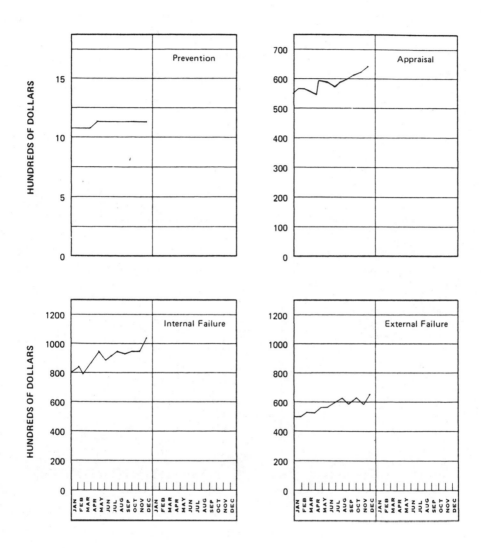

Figure 5

15

Quality Costs Related to Bases

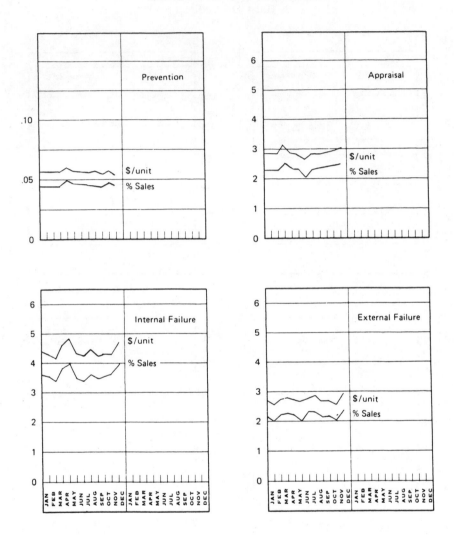

Figure 6

Finding The Problem Areas

Figures 5 & 6 show increases in the total dollars spent in all cost categories. Costs are stable when related to the measurement bases, except for internal failure. The internal failure costs have increased slightly over the 12-month period. This is an indication that further analysis of internal failure costs should be made. The technique most often used for further analysis is the Pareto analysis.

Pareto Analysis

The *Pareto analysis* technique involves listing the factors that contribute to the problem and ranking them according to the magnitude of their contribution. In most situations, a relatively small number of causes or sources will contribute a relatively large percentage of the total costs. To produce the greatest improvement, effort should be spent on reducing costs coming from the largest contributors. In the example, the largest contributor to the total costs and the one showing an increasing trend is internal failure. Figure 7 is a Pareto distribution showing the costs contributed by each element included in internal failure costs.

Two elements, scrap and remedial engineering, account for 69% of total internal failure costs. Pareto analysis can be used to determine where the scrap and remedial engineering costs are coming from. The distribution in Figure 8 shows that two departments in the shop account for 59% of the scrap charges. Figure 9 shows that 83% of the remedial engineering charges are being generated by two design engineering sections.

These distributions are typical of the ones which should be found in any company. Using this sequence of techniques, high cost contributors can be identified and targeted for corrective action attention. In this example, a 10% reduction in internal failure costs by only the two highest cost contributors would mean a $75,000 cost reduction:

($450,000 [scrap] + $300,000 [remedial engineering]) × 10% = $75,000

Objectives such as this are realistic and can be obtained if you know where to look. The Pareto analysis technique will reveal this information.

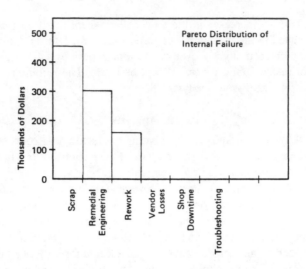

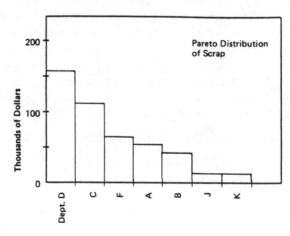

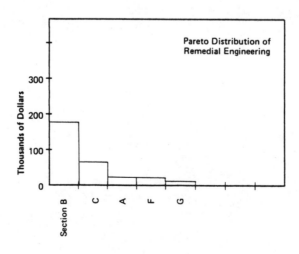

Figure 7

QUALITY COSTS ANALYSIS EXAMPLE

About the Operation

Last year, sales for the Transmotor Division of PQC Co. were approximately $25 million consisting of about 90% industrial customers and 10% government contracts. Profits after taxes were $1.2 million.

Sales increased steadily from $1.5 million to $2.6 million. This increase was due to the introduction and wide acceptance of a new product design. The new product was not only more reliable, but cost less to produce. With a sizeable amount of the new product in inventory at the start of last year, the production rate was not increased until the second quarter.

During the year, a recently hired quality control engineer started working on analysis of the quality program. He was able to improve systems and procedures, but since the middle of last year high rejection rates on the new product (both at final assembly and on parts) forced him to spend most of his time attempting to solve some of the problems causing the high rejection rates.

The division's Quality Control Manager, Carl Harris, has heard about the quality costs management technique and wants to see if it can benefit his division. Carl has attended several ASQC conferences and seminars and was able to talk with quality control managers of companies that make a product line similar to his. From what he can determine, it appears that quality costs between 4 and 6% of gross sales billed are common in companies making similar products. He is not sure, however, which cost elements are included in his competitor's costs. A rough calculation of his division's costs for last year's month of October reveals the following figures:

Prevention	$ 1,000
Appraisal	100,000
Internal Failure	36,000
External Failure	27,000
	$164,000

Carl's first attempt at establishing a quality engineering program began over a year and half ago with the hiring of an ASQC Certified Quality Engineer. Improvement of inspection methods and solutions to a few chronic quality problems have since enabled Carl to reassign several inspectors and cover the increased production load without increasing the number of inspectors in the last three quarters of the previous year. To date, there is still a considerable amount of 100% inspection being done, however, and Carl believes that more of the inspection process can be eliminated by upgrading the efficiency of the manufacturing process.

The cause of the present high rejection rate on the new product is not really known, and there is a considerable amount of "finger pointing" going on. Manufacturing blames a faulty design and the purchase of bad material; design engineering claims that the existing tolerances are not being met and that parts are being mishandled before they get to the assembly area.

Carl decides to find out which departments are the high cost contributors by setting up a quality costs program.

Starting the Program

The first decision the Quality Control Manager must make is on the unit to be covered by the study. Since there is no breakdown by profit center within the division, it is decided that the entire division will be included in the study.

The next thing the Quality Control Manager does is discuss the concept and proposed program with the Controller and requests his aid in the initial study and future reporting. The Controller is skeptical of the program, but he does agree to provide costs on those elements which are compiled and used for other purposes. The Controller also agrees to provide personnel to aid in compiling other element costs as the need arises.

This done, the elements to be studied must be selected. The elements shown on pages 21 and 22 are selected as those most representative of the Transmotor Division operation. It is found that there are no separate accounts for some of the elements and that estimates must be made for those items. In some cases, this requires splitting amounts in a general account according to an esitmated fraction of that account which should be charged to the element. Some estimating can best be done by counting the number of people working at such tasks as rework and sorting. Work sampling is also a valuable technique for such estimating. After deciding on the cost sources to use for each element, a detailed first study can be made. For the Transmotor Division, it was decided to collect data for the entire preceding year. This data is shown on pages 21 and 22.

The actual costs for each category are graphed in Figure 8.

Quality Costs Analysis Example

TOTAL QUALITY COSTS
TRANSMOTOR DIVISION

ELEMENTS	Jan.	Feb.	Mar.	Apr.	May	June	July	Aug.	Sept.	Oct.	Nov.	Dec.	Total
PREVENTION													
Quality Planning	500	550	400	300	350	250	0	200	250	0	100	100	3,000
Data Analysis and Corrective Action	500	500	600	700	650	750	250	800	760	1,000	900	900	8,300
Planning By Other Functions	600	400	700	750	700	650	650	650	600	700	700	650	7,750
Development of Measurement & Control Equipment	0	50	0	0	0	0	0	0	0	0	0	0	50
Training	0	0	0	0	0	0	0	0	250	0	0	0	250
Quality System Audits	0	0	0	0	0	0	0	0	0	0	0	0	
Other Prevention Expense	200	250	250	200	375	190	750	260	460	225	190	220	3,570
Total Prevention Costs	1,800	1,750	1,950	1,950	2,075	1,840	1,650	1,910	2,310	1,925	1,890	1,870	22,920
APPRAISAL													
Inspection & Test- Purchased Material	5,200	5,000	5,950	4,920	5,900	6,010	3,900	6,410	7,125	6,500	6,400	7,450	70,765
Laboratory Acceptance Testing	925	925	925	925	925	925	925	925	925	925	925	925	11,100
Maint. & Calibration of Equipment	3,840	3,840	3,840	3,840	3,840	3,840	3,840	3,840	3,840	3,840	3,840	3,840	46,080
Depreciation of Capital Equipment	695	695	695	695	695	695	695	695	695	695	695	695	8,340
Inspection	52,300	53,250	52,275	52,325	51,250	53,200	48,875	51,450	52,050	52,725	51,400	50,575	621,675
Testing	29,120	30,950	30,050	28,425	29,350	31,940	30,125	35,830	35,750	38,700	43,525	44,100	407,865
Set-Up of Inspection and Test	Included in "Inspection" and "Testing"												
Process & Product Audits	0	0	0	0	0	0	0	0	0	0	0	0	
Checking Labor	2,710	2,805	2,740	3,117	3,240	3,120	3,250	3,325	3,390	3,470	3,515	3,570	38,252
Inspection & Test Material	475	80	316	940	510	425	270	317	430	525	130	100	4,518
Outside Endorsement	0	0	0	0	0	0	0	0	0	0	0	0	
Personnel Qualification	0	0	0	30	0	0	0	0	0	30	0	0	60
Review of Test & Inspection Data	0	0	0	0	0	0	0	0	0	0	0	0	
Field Testing & Inspection	0	0	0	0	0	0	0	0	0	0	0	0	
Accumulation of Cost Data	0	0	0	0	0	0	0	0	0	0	0	0	
Total Appraisal Costs	95,265	97,545	96,791	95,217	95,710	100,155	91,880	102,792	104,205	107,410	110,430	111,255	1,208,655

21

TOTAL QUALITY COSTS
TRANSMOTOR DIVISION

ELEMENTS	Jan.	Feb.	Mar.	Apr.	May	June	July	Aug.	Sept.	Oct.	Nov.	Dec.	Total
INTERNAL FAILURE													
Scrap – Division Caused	25,170	15,025	19,112	18,997	28,040	33,980	9,060	20,050	22,150	18,220	27,110	24,140	261,054
Rework – Division Caused	5,200	6,150	9,210	4,925	9,010	6,020	7,800	10,500	12,250	10,875	12,900	12,040	103,880
Supplier Caused Losses	1,200	1,099	1,248	1,170	1,370	2,715	1,110	1,795	1,745	1,890	1,375	2,160	18,877
Troubleshooting	2,080	1,975	2,125	2,020	2,115	2,170	2,050	2,265	2,450	2,645	2,725	2,945	27,565
Retest and Reinspection	Not Separated from Inspection Costs												
Remedial Engineering	4,200	4,250	7,125	8,010	7,850	9,100	10,460	13,610	12,990	13,060	11,550	13,510	115,715
Substandard Product Costs	0	0	0	0	0	0	0	0	0	0	0	0	0
Shop Down Time	Not Identifiable												
Extra Production Operations	Not Identifiable												
Total Internal Failure Costs	37,850	28,499	35,820	35,122	48,385	53,985	30,480	48,220	51,585	46,690	55,660	54,795	527,091
EXTERNAL FAILURE													
Product Warranty	19,670	22,300	22,960	24,850	22,100	20,990	20,500	19,550	18,850	20,110	18,900	19,750	250,530
Returned Product Costs	1,800	1,800	1,800	1,800	1,800	1,800	1,800	1,800	1,800	1,800	1,800	1,800	21,600
Field Service	7,100	7,100	7,100	7,100	7,100	7,100	7,100	7,100	7,100	7,100	7,100	7,100	85,200
Total External Failure Costs	28,570	31,200	31,860	33,750	31,000	29,890	29,400	28,450	27,750	29,010	27,800	28,650	357,330
Total Quality Costs	163,485	158,994	166,421	166,039	177,170	185,870	153,410	181,372	185,850	185,035	195,780	196,570	2,115,996
Measurement Bases													
1. Gross Sales Billed	1,525,000	1,420,500	1,872,500	1,810,200	1,798,400	1,896,750	2,086,550	2,314,640	2,402,500	2,276,550	2,697,540	2,625,400	24,726,530
2. Factory Hours	82,650	83,152	82,164	81,245	82,360	91,200	83,750	96,750	112,500	115,750	115,700	91,250	1,118,471
3. Cost of Units Shipped	1,225,000	1,315,500	1,275,250	1,095,650	1,080,975	1,205,620	1,125,050	1,397,450	1,334,150	1,400,500	1,602,930	1,625,625	15,683,700

Quality Costs Analysis Example

Internal failure, appraisal and the total costs show an upward trend, as would be expected in a period of increasing activity. Prevention costs haven't changed, but external failure costs peaked during the first half of the year and now appear to be leveling off. The next step is to find appropriate measures of business activity to which to relate the data. The quality manager chose gross sales billed, cost of units shipped to inventory and factory hours. These data were collected from accounting and industrial engineering, and costs from each category were expressed as a fraction of the bases chosen. Graphs of these fractions are shown on the following three pages.

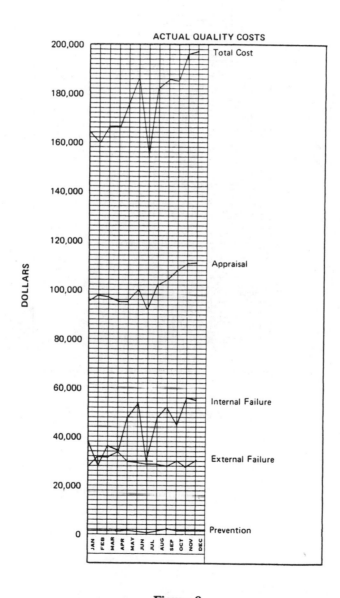

Figure 8

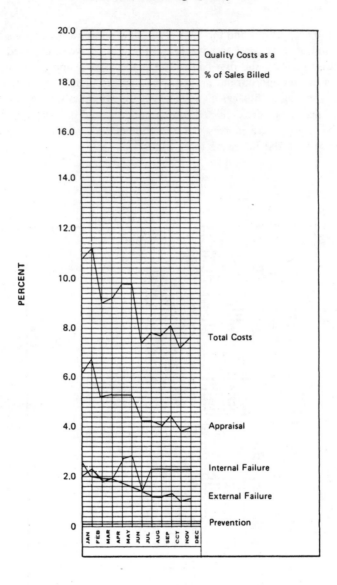

Figure 8 (con't)

Quality Costs Analysis Example

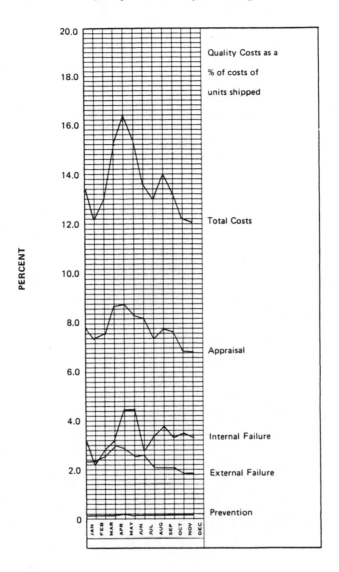

Figure 8 (con't)

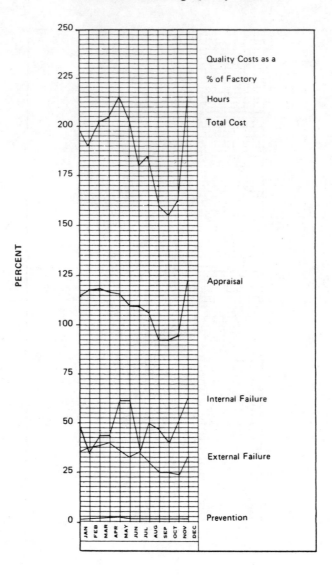

Figure 8 (con't)

26

Quality Costs Analysis Example

When expressed as a fraction of sales, total costs, appraisal, and external failure show a downward trend while prevention and internal failure are essentially unchanged. These trends, however, are not valid ones, since sales in this case is not a good measure of the kind of activity producing the costs. Most of product billed was coming out of warehouse stocks for the first half of the year. The ratio plots using factory hours show roughly the same trends as the ones using standard costs. Total costs peaked about midyear and appear to be going down. Appraisal and external failure cost ratios show a slight upward trend. Prevention has not changed. This analysis invites attention to the increasing internal failure cost ratio. Looking at this more closely, it is found that the major contributors to the increase are rework, supplier caused losses, and remedial engineering. The largest dollar contributor is scrap. Graphs of internal failure costs as fractions of standard costs are shown in Figure 9.

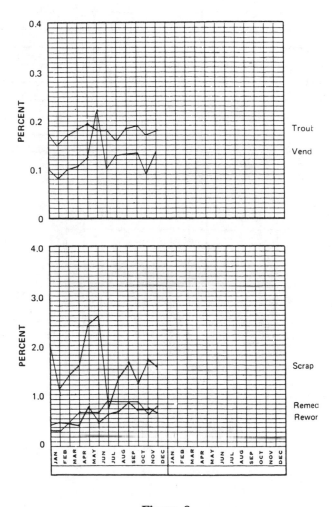

Figure 9

This leads to the question, "Where are these costs being generated?" The quality control manager requested a breakdown of the source of the three largest dollar contributors to the internal failure: scrap, rework and remedial engineering. Cost of these three elements represents 91% of the total internal failure costs. It was found that three sections of the shop (Winding, Feeder 5) generated 82% of the scrap during the last year. Three sections (Winding, Assembly and Feeder 1) contributed 80% of the rework charges, and one model (Model T) accounted for 60% of the remedial engineering. Figure 10 contains graphs of these cost breakdowns.

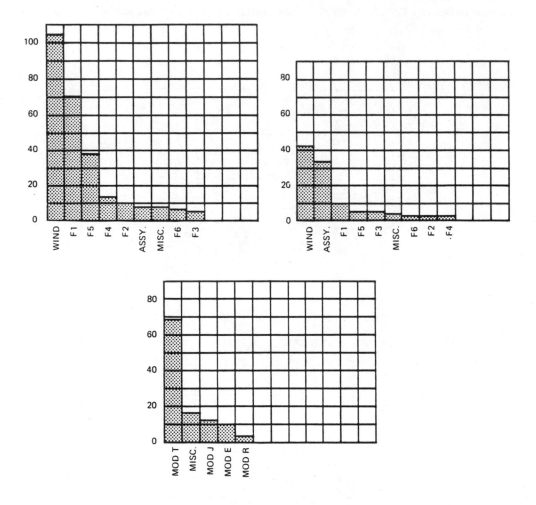

Figure 10

Quality Costs Analysis Example

The quality control manager now has enough information to begin to develop a corrective action program. To be effective, it must involve both the manufacturing manager and the engineering manager since the elements which are the largest contributors to internal failure costs are the responsibility of these functional managers. He must also look at costs which are his own responsibility, prevention and appraisal. Reductions in overall costs will require a program of cooperative effort. A meeting is held with the responsible functional managers at which the quality control manager presents the results of his study and analysis to this point. Each manager is asked for his views on the program and whether he feels that the costs for which he is responsible could be reduced and if so, by how much. At this meeting, objectives and plans for achievement of them are requested from each responsible manager.

The initial report contains all data and graphs generated in the study, the objectives for cost reduction and plans for reaching the objective. Objectives developed by the management team are:

1. Reduce the overall quality costs to 6.7% of sales billed within one year.
2. Reduce appraisal costs to 3.3% of gross sales billed within two years, and to 3.6% within one year.
3. Reduce internal failure costs to 1.8% of sales within one year.
4. Maintain external failure costs at no more than 1.1% of sales.

Action programs for attainment of these objectives are:

1. Hire an additional quality control engineer charged with the responsibility of identification of the causes of high cost problems and coordination of corrective action.
2. Reassign the present quality engineer to the task of finding less costly ways of inspection and test, and ways of elimination of 100% inspection.
3. Set up committees consisting of representatives of manufacturing, engineering and quality control in the sections of the shop having high scrap and rework costs. Set objectives for reduction and report progress regularly.
4. Set up a task force to determine the cause of the excessive remedial engineering costs on the Model T unit. Set an objective for reduction of the costs and report progress regularly.
5. Determine the causes of the highest field problems. If shop caused, assign to the shop committees for action. If caused by design or application, assign to the task force for attention. Set objectives and require reporting.
6. Issue a quality cost report each quarter showing performance against objectives, discussing major problem areas, and plans for reduction of costs.

At this point we leave the Transmotor quality control manager with the thought that he is well on his way to elimination of a lot of his headaches and making the quality control function a profit contributor for the division.

THE TEAM APPROACH

Once a problem has been identified and reported and the involved personnel are committed for action the job is started but far from complete. The efforts of people involved must be planned, coordinated, scheduled, implemented, and followed-up. Problems can normally be thought of as one of two types; those which one individual or department can correct with little or no outside help and those requiring coordinated action from several activities in the organization. Examples of the first type of problem are operator-controllable defects, design errors, and inspection errors. Examples of the second type are product performance problems for which a cause is not known, defects caused by a combination of factors not under the control of one department, and field failures of unknown cause.

To attack and solve problems of the first type, an elaborate system is not required. Most can and should be resolved at the working level with the foreman, the engineer, or other responsible parties. Usually, the working personnel of these departments have sufficient authority to enact corrective action, within defined limits, without specific approval of their superiors. If documentation of such problems is desired, the use of a "Quality Improvement Project" is recommended. Figure 11 illustrates a copy of this form along with instructions for completing it.

Unfortunately, problems of the second type are normally the most costly and are not as easily solved. Causes of such problems may be numerous and unknown. Solution may require action from several sources. The investigation of the problem and the planning of its solution must be coordinated and scheduled to assure that effective action is taken. One of the best devices for doing this is the quality improvement committee. Working with the data and problem analysis reports and headed by an individual who is interested in solving the problems, this committee develops the plan, and then coordinates and schedules the investigation and action. It has been found that an interested individual with line responsibility (i.e. General Foreman) makes the best chairman for such a group. Each project should be docketed and action scheduled. Meetings should be held regularly and minutes published.

Frequency of the meetings should be determined considering the seriousness and number of problems to be considered. The Quality Problem Docket form (Figure 12) is recommended for docketing the problem, planning the steps necessary to investigate and solve it, assigning responsibility, and calculating the resulting savings.

Frequent prodding and pushing by the quality engineer are often needed to assure that the program remains effective. Meetings may get postponed, action delayed, or discouragement may set in when the program appears to be making little progress. This tests the salesmanship and organizing ability of the quality engineer to the fullest. Some techniques which have worked well in reviving efforts are:

1. Individual discussions with committee members or their supervisors to discover the reason for delays and lack of interest.
2. The introduction of fresh projects with a high potential return.
3. Obtaining statements of interest in the committee activities from higher management.
4. Changing personnel on the committee to obtain a fresh outlook on problems or to replace a member who has lost interest.
5. Bringing in technical personnel to develop new approaches (such as designed experiments) to the solution of the problem or to analyze the design, tooling, or control systems for contributing factors.

The Quality Problem Forms (Figures 12 and 13) are recommended for docketing the problem.

31

REDUCING FAILURE COSTS

This section discusses four steps to an effective corrective action program and describes some techniques which have been found to work in accomplishing each step. The four steps are:

1. Make all persons concerned aware of the problem and its possible causes.
2. Create a desire in others to solve the mutual problem.
3. Plan and carry out a logical investigation of the problem with others involved.
4. Follow-up on action taken.

Making People Aware of Problems and Possible Causes

The quality engineer should personally investigate the problem to the extent necessary to define the problem and uncover some of the possible causes. In the process, he may become convinced that he has discovered the basic cause and can take action or request action without involving those not directly concerned. In many cases, a number of possible causes will be apparent from the initial investigation and the quality engineer must interest others in taking action. A most effective means of doing this has been found to be regular reports accompanying the inspection and test data summaries which briefly describe the problems, the investigation of them to date, the causes or possible causes of the problems, and corrective measures taken or needed to solve them. The description of the problem should include its effect on costs, schedule, or product quality.

Quality performance reports should be prepared in a clear and concise format. They should be sent to the people who can pursue the investigations suggested in the report and who have sufficient authority to initiate action to correct the identified quality problems. The responsibility for corrective action, as well as the date by which the work is scheduled for completion, should be clearly identified in the report. The report should also include a review of the progress made in correcting earlier problems.

Quality performance reports should be sent to other departments and to higher management personnel because these reports:

- Provide management with information needed for programming, budgeting, and following projects through to completion.
- Keep management informed of the status of quality.
- Reveal the magnitude of the quality problems in each of the major areas of the quality control program.
- Provide a means of comparing the quality performance achieved with the performance objectives.
- Give early indication of quality trends in each area of the plant, providing time for action before the trends become major problems.
- Provide before-and-after comparisons that permit evaluation of the effects that major changes have on processes and systems.
- Identify the kinds of defects that have been most common or costly.
- Identify areas that have had a consistently good quality performance which may justify reductions in quality control effort and result in a consequent reduction in quality cost.

Each quality performance report should summarize information, emphasizing what is significant, pointing out trends, and citing instance of good performance. The report should also call attention to poor performance that needs immediate attention. Graphs and charts are an excellent way to make this information stand out. In general, it is not necessary to include all of the detailed data as a part of the report, but if the need arises to do so, the data should be effectively organized. The report should enable the persons receiving it to grasp the significance of the information and the type of corrective measures that are required.

Creating a Desire to Solve The Problem

Most quality managers who never accomplish the goals set for them are the victims of an inability to solve the chronic "quality" problems existing in their companies. The ironic thing, however, is that the causes of these problems are not normally ones which they can correct. The causes may be bad design, improper tooling, improper manufacturing sequences, improper application or a host of others, most of which are correctable only by someone else. The quality manager's task is, therefore, to get someone else to do something about the problems. Once this fact is realized the quality manager can set about designing a corrective action program which will make others in the organization aware of the problems and create a desire for solving them.

Most people don't like to repair defective work. Foremen generally have a feeling for the effect that rework and scrap are having on their productivity and schedule and they do not like it. The shop superintendent and engineering manager normally react positively when factual data indicate that there is a costly, time consuming problem. With all these factors which favor a program for correcting quality problems, why are effective corrective action programs so scarce?

Normally, it is for one or more of the following reasons:

1. People are unaware that a problem exists. They don't realize the profit and schedule impact of rejections and scrap.
2. They are convinced by past management or staff performance that even if a problem is reported, nothing will be done about it.
3. A condition has been allowed to exist so long that it is accepted as a way of operating.
4. Lack of proper balance of top management attention between schedule, cost, and quality.
5. Personal relationships between quality control and other parts of the organization are such that problems cannot be rationally discussed.

The techniques recommended in this guide will not overcome all the roadblocks listed; however, they have been found to be some of the best approaches to achieving an effective program.

Simply reporting a problem is not enough. The quality engineer must first develop the confidence of the people with whom he is working by demonstrating his interest in solving problems and his ability to get solutions. He must assure that the system for collecting the data and the people reporting the data are providing factual information. He must assure that his analysis of the data and initial problem investigation are based on sound engineering approaches to the problem. He must assure that the solution of the problem will result in a cost reduction. All this effort can be ineffective, however, if he fails to stimulate others to take action to solve a problem. This is a selling job. He must sell himself, his program, and the fact that the problem is serious enough to warrant spending the time and money necessary to solve it. He must appeal to the primary interests of the people who have to do something to help solve the problem.

To gain support from general management and functional department management, the problem should be stated in management terms. The cost of the problems, the amount of effort needed for solution, and the savings from solution should be estimated and stated in the reports to these managers. The engineering department must be convinced that the quality engineer knows what he is talking about from a technical standpoint. Engineers can often be stimulated to correct a design problem when it is demonstrated that the problem is one which could affect either the cost of producing the product or product reliability. When the problem involves tooling the manufacturing engineers must be convinced that a problem is costly enough to warrant changing the tooling or method of manufacture. The first line supervisor must be convinced that the quality engineer can actually do something about getting a solution and that solving the problem will improve the efficiency of his operation. The operator must be shown that problems and suggestions for improvement brought to the attention of the quality engineer receive attention and that action will result. As mentioned earlier, people generally don't like to do rework. A promise of rework reduction will help sell the program to operating people. If the problem is causing customer complaints, selling the need for solution to anyone in the organization should be easier.

There are cases where even the best selling job will fall on deaf ears for any number of reasons. Consider the possibility that your proposal was not accepted because it may be unsound. If you are still convinced that the solution of the problem will contribute to the profitability of the business and that you have a workable program for solving it, there are ways around roadblocks.

When programs are successfully executed, give credit liberally in follow-up reports when it is due. Be especially kind to those who may have opposed the idea initially but, when pressured did make a contribution to the solution. It is much easier to enlist the future aid of those who have been given credit for a successful previous effort.

Planning for Corrective Action

Problems identified as a result of analysis of quality data should be docketed for corrective action by some formal means. Problems which can be solved by one individual or department can be documented on a simple form which provides space for describing the problem and the corrective action to be taken and some means of following up on the problem if action is not taken. Figure 11 is a copy of such a form. Instructions for its use are provided below the form.

When problems are of such a nature that action is required by more than one individual or department to solve it, or when a long term or expensive solution is required, a more elaborate docket form is needed. Figures 12 and 13 are examples of such forms with instructions for their use.

QUALITY IMPROVEMENT PROJECT

DEPT.	DEPT. SUPV. OF QUALITY CONTROL		PROJECT NO.
MFG. FOREMAN	WORK TO BE DONE BY (NAME)	DATE DOCKETED	DATE TO BE COMPLETED

DESCRIPTION OF TROUBLE (PARTS, ASSEMBLIES OR OPERATION INVOLVED — BE SPECIFIC)

FOREMAN'S SIGNATURE	DATE

PROJECT COMPLETED ☐   PROJECT NOT COMPLETED ☐

If promised completion date is not met, state why _____

DEPT. SUPV., QUAL. CONTROL	DATE

TO: MR. _____ MANAGER OF MANUFACTURING

The above project has not been completed on the promised date. This copy is forwarded for your information and action.

DIV. SUPV.
QUAL. CONT. _____ DATE _____

IT COSTS LESS TO MAKE IT RIGHT THE FIRST TIME

Figure 11

Instructions for the use of the "Quality Improvement Project." (QIP)

1. *Department* — Enter the department experiencing the problem.
2. *Department Supv. of Quality Control* — Enter the name of the cognizant Q. C. Supervisor. In most situations this will be the originator of the form, although a QIP may be initiated by others.
3. *Project No.* — Sequentially number the projects and enter the number in this space.
4. *Manufacturing Foreman* — Enter the name of the manufacturing foreman for the affected area.
5. *Work to be done by* — Enter the name of the individual who is to be responsible for correcting the problem.
6. *Date Docketed* — Self explanatory.
7. *Date to be Completed* — Enter the date by which correction is requested.
8. *Description of Trouble* — Describe the problem in specific terms. Include actual dimensions, rejection rates, dollar losses due to the problem, etc. Include all information pertinent to the problem.

9. *Corrective Action* — This section is to be completed by the individual doing the work or his supervisor. Specific steps to be taken to solve the problem should be stated and dates for accomplishment must be given. This section is to be signed by the supervisor responsible for taking the action.
10. All projects are to be followed to completion by quality control. If promised dates are not met, the reasons should be determined and entered in the space provided.
11. Space is provided at the bottom of the form for referring unresolved problems to higher management. This should be done by quality control, when it is apparent that effective action is not being taken to resolve a costly problem.

QUALITY PROBLEM DOCKET

Docket Number	Docket Title		
Product Affected	Departments Affected		Indv. Resp. for Coordination
Problem Description			
Estimated Date Problem Began:			
Probable Cause			

Loss Due to Problem	In-Plant	In-Field	Total
Loss to Date	————	————	————
Projected Loss if not Corrected	————	————	————

Corrective Action			
Required On:	Current Production	Inventory	Product in Field
Date Scheduled	————	————	————
Date Corrected	————	————	————

Initiated By _____ Date _____

Figure 12

Instructions for the Use of the "Quality Problem Docket."

1. *Docket Number* — Assign a number to each docket and enter in this space.
2. *Docket Title* — Title the docket to be descriptive of the problem. Enter in this space.
3. *Product Affected* — Enter the product line(s) affected by the problem.

4. *Department Affected* — Enter the factory departments affected by the problem.
5. *Individual Responsible for Coordination* — Enter the name of the individual in the organization who is responsible for coordinating the efforts directed at solving the problem. This individual will normally be the chairman of the quality improvement committee following the problem.
6. *Problem Description* — Describe the problem in as much detail as possible. Include rejection levels, effect of production flow, effect on product performance, and any other factors which may be affected by the problem. Do not include cost information in the description as it is covered by another section of the docket form. Use attachments if necessary to completely describe the problem.
7. *Estimated Date Problem Began* — Self explanatory.
8. *Probable Cause* — Enter the probable cause or causes of the problem. If causes are unknown, so state. List all known possible causes.
9. *Loss Due to Problem* — Enter all dollar losses incurred because of the problem and the projected losses if the problem is not corrected. Loss amounts should be stated as dollars per month, dollars per year, or cost related to some other base.
10. *Corrective Action* — Indicate the extent of corrective action needed and the dates on which action is scheduled. When action is taken, enter the dates correction is made. In most cases, these dates must be determined by the problem solving team at the same time as the action plan is formulated.

QUALITY PROBLEM CORRECTIVE ACTION PLAN

Event No.	Corrective Action Event	Event Responsibility	Date Completed		Status Review	
			Schedule	Actual	Date	Comments

Quality Cost Savings		
Cost Category	Projected	Actual
Appraisal Cost Reduction		
Internal Failure Cost Reduction		
External Failure Cost Reduction		
Other (Explain)		
Cost Savings		
Cost of Problem Solution		
Net Savings		

Signature of Responsible Individuals

Figure 13

1. *Quality Problem Corrective Action Plan* — This portion of the docket form is designed for planning a step-by-step program for investigating and solving the problem. Each event necessary for the problem solution should be listed along with the name of the individual responsible for its accomplishment and a scheduled completion date. Also provided are spaces in which actual completion dates and results of periodic status reviews are recorded. As problem analysis and investigation proceeds, the plan will often need revision because of new findings or changing conditions. When this happens, the revised plan should be documented by changing the original on the docket form or by attaching a new form. Responsibility and scheduled completion dates must be indicated on the revised schedule.

2. *Quality Cost Savings* — Each project should be evaluated to determine what the projected savings will be and the results of problem solution should be evaluated by the resultant savings. All quality cost savings should be included. In addition, any reductions in such things as direct labor and material, inventory, material handling, etc. should be included. The costs of problem solution include such things as direct labor costs for employees working to solve the problem, material costs, travel, consultants, etc. Subtract the cost of problem solution from total savings to obtain net savings.

3. *Signatures of Responsible Individual* — Each individual who has responsibility for any event in the corrective action plan should sign.

Follow-Up

The first step in effective follow-up to corrective action is measurement of the results. This requires use of an effective data collection system — the same one used to identify the problems. This means that collection and reporting of quality data must be a continuous process so that changes, both good and bad, can be detected. The results of problem solution should be expressed in dollars. Savings should be calculated using the space on the back of the "Quality Problem Docket" and documented as a part of the company's cost improvement program.

Results of the problem solution should be reported to all concerned using the same report used for problem reporting. Credit should be given liberally for all contributions to problem solutions. Where shop personnel have contributed, they should be given credit for their part and informed of the results.

Once improvements have been made, the problem then becomes one of assuring that the gains made will be permanent. Holding the improved quality levels is a vital need, although provision for this is often overlooked. Lacking provision for holding the new gains, it is common to see improvement trends reverse themselves and head toward former levels. A file of open problem dockets should be maintained and reviewed periodically. After action is taken to solve a problem, a review should be made to assure that the action is effective.

Reducing Failure Costs Check List

1. Are the causes of high cost elements known and reported to those responsible for action?

1a. Are scrap and rework charges reported to the manufacturing foreman in such a way that he can identify the vital few high cost contributors and take corrective action?

1b. Are remedial engineering charges reported to the responsible engineering supervisor in a form which allows him to quickly find the high cost contributors and take action.

1c. Are supplier caused losses reported to purchasing and the receiving inspection department so action can be taken?

2. Are defects found in assembly areas reported to sections or suppliers responsible and is corrective action taken?

3. Are the basic causes of defects found and corrected, or does the action taken tend to be to screen out the defectives after they are made?

4. Is non-conforming material salvaged where economical?

5. Are there areas where a high rejection rate has become a way of life and little effort is being made to correct the situation?

6. Is the corrective action program broad enough to demand design or tooling changes, if that is what is needed to prevent the production of defectives?

7. Is there a coordinated quality improvement effort involving all the necessary departments?

8. Does the quality improvement effort include regular meetings, docketed projects with completion dates, and written progress reports?

9. Does the program have the continuing interest and support of the functional department managers and the general manager? If not, what must be done to gain that interest and support?

10. Are causes of high cost field problems identified and is action being taken on them to prevent recurrence?

11. Are warranty charges audited for validity and action taken as necessary?

12. Are returned products economically handled, repaired and returned to the customer?

13. Are clear field performance objectives set to assure a continuing controlled or reduced cost?

PREVENTION OF QUALITY COSTS

Up to this point, we have been discussing ways to find and solve problems which are already costing money. How much better it would be if those problems could have been prevented from happening! Prevention activities are of two basic types — those related to employee attitudes and resulting approach to their jobs, and those formal techniques which identify potential problems early in the product cycle and eliminate them before they become expensive.

Employee attitudes toward quality are determined in large part by their beliefs about what is really wanted by their boss and higher management of the business and by the degree to which they are personally involved in the improvement program. Management's commitment to quality improvement must be visible to all employees. The first line supervisors play key roles in a successful quality improvement program. They should thoroughly understand and be involved with the elements affecting their people. Some specific suggestions for involving all employees are:

- Employees should be aware of all aspects of the program affecting them or their work. Planned verbal communications, posters, charts, reports, and displays have all been found to be effective.
- There should be a way for each employee to present his ideas for quality improvement. Each idea should be properly evaluated and the employees should be told of the results.
- Involving employees in goal setting sometimes results in higher goals than would have been set otherwise.
- Good ideas and achievement of performance in excess of established goals should be publically recognized. There are many ways to recognize achievement, but remember, it must have been honestly earned, have meaning and value, and be properly presented and publicized.

Formal programs for preventing deficiencies in the product have been used by some companies for many years, but, unfortunately, are not in general use. Some examples of these programs are:

- New product verification programs which require that new products be thoroughly reviewed, inspected, tested and proven prior to release for quantity production.
- Design review programs requiring a thorough and detailed review of new or significantly changed designs by a group representing all segments of the organization.
- Supplier selection programs which require an evaluation of the potential supplier's ability to supply the required quality before an order is placed with him.
- Reliability testing to discover problems before they cause high field failure costs.
- Thorough training and testing of employees placed on critical jobs.

Developing effective methods for doing each job right the first time is important to a continuing quality improvement program.

Prevention in Marketing

Quality assurance in marketing is a new concept, but the problems it can help reduce are old ones. We are in business to provide products and services which satisfy customer needs. The extent to which we do this is a measure of our quality performance. Marketing inputs are vital to determining what those needs are and how well we are satisfying them.

Marketing's quality responsibilities include:

- Accurately determining the customer's quality requirements.
- Assuring that prices reflect unusual requirements.
- Assuring that customer requirements are accurately reflected in internal ordering information and design specification.
- Establishing with others in the organization, quality standards for products not completely specified by the customer.
- Participating in the product development and verification cycle to the extent necessary to assure that the required product characteristics are included in the product.
- Honestly advertising and marketing the products to assure that the customer knows what he is purchasing.
- Obtaining complete information on product performance from customers.
- Reporting product performance information to those responsible for solving the problems.
- Following and participating in the corrective action programs on chronic field problems.
- Administering warranty claims honestly and fairly, but with enough controls to assure that such costs are not excessive.

Prevention in Design

Many of the most costly problems with products are caused by inadequate designs. Many manufacturing, assembly, test and product performance problems often called "quality" problems have some root causes in the way the parts or the assembly have been designed. These problems certainly are "quality" problems, but quality programs often do not contain elements to deal with them. Engineering has very significant quality responsibilities and must have controls within their operating systems and procedures to assure that design and drafting work is done right the first time, just as there are such controls for machinists. Engineering responsibilities for quality include:

- Designing a product which is safe for its intended use and, if built according to the design, will perform reliably for its intended life.
- Designing a product which can be profitably manufactured.
- Designing a product which will satisfy the customer's needs.
- Preparing drawings and specifications which clearly and accurately describe the design and the quality criteria for it.
- Actively participating in problem investigations and promptly correcting design caused deficiencies.

Many "tools" are available for use in a design phase quality program. Most can and should be administered within the engineering department. The control elements in the systems for design should be coordinated with the other elements of the company's quality program to produce effective overall control.

Prevention in Quality Assurance

The quality function should review contractual customer specifications. Quality requirements must be determined. The review should concentrate on these elements:

- Quality assurance system provisions. Are they clear and complete?
- Specialized types of specifications (military, NASA, etc.) Are they acceptable?

- The quality levels and quality standards required. Is the product capable of meeting them?
- What design controls are needed.
- Documentation and reports. Is the subject matter clearly specified? Will the information be available when the report is to be written?
- Tests and inspection. Can we perform them with the equipment we now have? Where should they be performed?
- Dimensional requirements of the product. Are we capable of meeting them?
- Special tests. Will additional or modified equipment be required?
- Data reporting and corrective action activities.
- Special government requirements. Do our present quality systems and procedures comply with these requirements or must they be modified?

Ambiguities and uncertainties must be resolved. Making assumptions about what a customer wants without checking with him to be sure can lead to quality problems and customer dissatisfaction. Care must be exercised when written specifications have been supplemented or expanded by discussions with the customer. There is always a danger of misinterpretation. The quality function should satisfy itself that customer requirements have not been misconstrued.

This is also the time to start the planning. Modifications or additions may be required in equipment, procedures, or instructions to comply with the quality requirements. For example, measured test data may be required by the customer but the standard testing is "go/no-go". Manufacturing information and test instructions must be modified to reflect this change. Also, if specialized quality equipment is required, it should be ordered promptly to assure that it is available for use at the required time. Early planning pays off. Schedule delays and added costs result from lack of timely planning.

Prevention Check List

1. Could additional effort in planning profitably reduce appraisal or failure costs?
2. Could audits be used instead of 100% or lot-by-lot inspection?
3. Could improved supplier selection and control programs reduce total costs?
4. Could design reviews be profitably used?
5. Are quality engineering programs designed to prevent defectives from being produced?
6. Is there a clearly stated, well-known division quality policy?
7. Are drawing and measuring instrument control programs in existence and effective?
8. Are training programs providing a profitable return? Do costs show that new ones are needed?

REDUCING APPRAISAL COSTS

The costs of appraisal sometimes approach half of the total quality costs. Although most quality cost improvement programs properly concentrate on reducing failure costs first, programs for appraisal cost improvement can also have a significant impact. This section discusses several techniques for improving these costs.

- Inspection & test planning
- Equipment & methods improvement
- Statistical process control
- Accuracy studies
- Decision analysis
- Work sampling

Inspection and Test Planning

Getting the most out of the available appraisal resources requires careful planning. Determining where control points should be and the amount of inspection and test, should be the job of professionals — not left to the judgment of the individual inspector or tester.

In-process controls are a vital part of a prevention oriented quality system. They provide a powerful means for reducing the incidence of defective finished product and for reducing quality costs. In addition, an effective in-process inspection system often makes it possible to reduce the amount of final inspection required. In-process inspection control involves inspections or verifications performed at significant stages of the manufacturing process. If defective parts or subassemblies are being produced, the trouble can be detected early and corrected before it affects the quality of the finished product. *The system must be efficiently designed so that every inspection will serve an essential purpose.* Accomplishing quality by excessive inspection is costly and may absorb the savings created by eliminating defective product.

Finished product requirements and inspection and test specifications, should be thoroughly reviewed during the development of the in-process inspections and controls. This review provides the quality engineer with the information needed to determine the type and degree of in-process inspection required at various stages of the manufacturing process or assembly operations. It also helps him select the kinds of in-process controls that will prevent the manufacture of defective product and yield the best economic return. A periodic review of the planned inspections and tests should be made to assure that the levels remain economical in light of quality history. This section of the guide briefly reviews five types of inspection and test controls and the advantages and disadvantages of each:

- Operator inspection
- 100% in-line inspection
- First piece inspection
- Patrol inspection
- In-process acceptance inspection

Operator Inspection

In-process controls can be enhanced by requiring an operator, stationed at a machine or at a processing station, to inspect his own work. The operator must be provided with proper gages and be instructed in their proper use. He should be trained to recognize when an item is unacceptable in appearance. His work standards should provide enough time to allow the inspection to be performed with reasonable care.

These are the advantages of operator inspection:

- The operator usually handles every piece coming off the line.
- He is thoroughly familiar with the item he is making.
- He is in a position to spot defects quickly and call for help to correct problems as soon as they appear.

One caution is that special care may be necessary for the operator to keep the records normally required for an effective inspection procedure.

100% In-Line Inspection

Inspection or testing may be carried out on a 100% basis at designated points in the manufacturing line. This type of inspection or testing is normally performed by inspection or test personnel. Its purpose is to screen out items that either do not conform to quality workmanship standards or are not likely to pass the finished product inspection.

The following are some of the advantages and disadvantages of 100% in-line inspection.

Advantages
- It saves the cost of further processing of a product that is likely to fail final inspection and test.
- It provides data on quality performance that can be used to take corrective action.

Disadvantages:
- The in-line inspection function may become a routine step in the manufacturing line and because the rejects are being screened out, there may be less emphasis on the prevention of defects.
- It tends to duplicate inspection and increase inspection costs.
- It is not 100% effective because performing 100% inspection does not guarantee that all of the defective items will be detected.

First-Piece Inspection

In first-piece inspection, several pieces at the beginning of every new run are inspected to determine whether the set-up has been properly made and whether the tooling is adequate. The sample should provide a complete check of the machine or operation set-up. If the machine has nine spindles, for instance, samples should be taken from each spindle. Usually, the first five pieces produced by the new set-up constitute a large enough sample.

The advantage of first-piece inspection is that since the items turned out by a process or operation are evaluated at the beginning of the run, any necessary correction can be made before the run is started. This saves the cost of defective material that would be produced if the correction were not made.

Patrol Inspection

The inspector patrols the operations at periodic intervals and inspects the items being produced. Since inspection is performed concurrently with the operation, patrol inspection can provide faster response than inspection after the item has been completed. When problems occur, the inspector can have action initiated to correct them before many defective items are made.

It is advantageous to use patrol inspection under the following conditions:

- When a process turns out a high percentage of defective products and requires frequent inspection.
- When a process is erratic and the operator is unable to do a thorough job of inspection.
- When there is a need to collect special detailed data on the performance of the process.
- When an audit of the process is required.

In-Process Acceptance Inspection

This is the classic type of inspection. All the items made at an operation in a given period of time are inspected together as a lot. They must be inspected before they are approved for release to the next operation. The inspector takes a sample from the lot and if the lot meets the specified quality level, it is accepted and released to the next operation. If it fails to meet the required level, it is rejected and held for disposition.

In-process acceptance inspection provides several advantages:

- It makes it possible to control the quality level at each successive stage of the manufacturing process.
- It provides data to use in preparing performance reports to help pinpoint problem areas.

On the other hand, it also has some limitations:

- It does not prevent defects since the inspection is performed after the items have been completed.
- It delays the movement of parts from one operation to the next.
- It is not easily applied to continuous processes because of the difficulty of forming lots without disrupting the continuity of production.

Of the five types of inspection, none is completely effective by itself. An efficiently designed inspection system requires several of them in combination. How they can best be combined to serve particular needs depends on an evaluation of the following factors:

- The cost of each type of inspection.
- The type of manpower each type requires; the amount and availability of manpower.
- The history of quality performance. Has the process been in control in the past? If the process has given little trouble, inspection need not be as extensive as when the process has been frequently out of control.
- The type of process. Is it continuous, or can the items produced be collected and inspected in batches?
- The stability and the capability of the process.
- The nature of the product characteristics being controlled. Are the characteristics critical or minor?

Improving Equipment and Methods

Many of the most profitable areas for savings of inspection and test costs lie in improved equipment and methods used to do the job. Since inspection and test are not usually measured and controlled to the extent production jobs are, they are not usually too efficient. Improvements can often be made by:

1. Providing equipment which can perform inspection and test tasks faster or without operators.
2. Building inspection or test devices into production equipment.
3. Designing improved record and reporting systems which require less time and effort.
4. Applying industrial engineering techniques to improve inspection and test station layouts and methods.

The first step in improving equipment and methods should be to find out where the high cost areas are, that is, where most of the effort is now being applied. Construct a Pareto distribution of the present costs. Then concentrate improvement efforts in the high cost areas. Any highly repetitive inspection or test operation should be considered a candidate for improvement. Once improvement possibilities have been identified, alternative methods should be sought and considered. Equipment suppliers, and other specialists are all good sources for information on techniques and equipment which have been found to be profitable in similar applications. Manufacturing and industrial engineering can often provide guidance on integrating inspection and tests into production equipment and on work measurement and station layouts. Use of computers and automatic data recorders should be considered to minimize data handling and analysis.

There are almost sure to be improvement opportunities of the types described in any quality control operation. Quality cost analysis can point them out and help to provide the needed justification for the initial expenses involved in new equipment or methods studies.

Statistical Process Control

Statistical Process Control (SPC) includes powerful tools for use in helping to achieve in-process control. These include capability studies, control charts, and sampling inspections. Powerful tools that can be used to help achieve in-process control are capability studies, control charts and sampling inspection.

A capability study shows whether a machine or process is inherently capable of turning out items that conform to specification. When all of the items inspected in the capability study fall within the specification, it is demonstrated that the machine is capable of meeting the requirements. The results of the study may even indicate that it is possible to reduce the amount of inspection without adversely affecting quality. On the other hand, a capability study may reveal that a certain percentage of the items will always exceed the tolerances of the specification. In this case, it may be necessary either to relax the tolerances or to acquire a machine that is capable of meeting them. Capability studies can also be used to indicate whether an increase or decrease in the machine or process setting is necessary to produce items within specification.

Control charts are another excellent tool for increasing the efficiency of the in-process control techniques. In any series of measurements, there is variation. Sometimes the variation is only the natural outcome of "constant causes" inherent in the process. In other situations there is also variation due to "assignable causes." In the first case, the variation is normal and the process should be left alone. In the second, the variation indicates that something has gone wrong with the process and action should be taken to correct it. The problem is to decide which type of variation is present.

Acceptance sampling techniques provide a means of measuring and controlling quality without the necessity of checking all the units produced. By using a sampling plan it is sometimes possible to significantly reduce the costs associated with appraisal while still maintaining adequate control.

Accuracy Studies

There are failure costs associated with incorrect quality decisions on the part of inspectors, testers, or operators. These can be due to:

1. Falsely rejecting acceptable material.
2. Falsely accepting rejectable material.

There are many plans which rate appraisal personnel in relation to these two errors. Perhaps the easiest to apply is one involving accuracy as a percent of defects correctly identified. This involves submitting a known number of good and bad units to an individual and rating his ability to correctly separate the units. The number of incorrect decisions is then multiplied by the cost of each wrong decision and an extension is made showing the cost implications.

Decision Analysis

In the early manufacturing of a new product (and in spite of good quality planning) the need for adjustment of measurement and test controls is generally revealed. This creates a need to analyze the effectiveness of decisions made on components, sub-assemblies and final product in terms of the earliest possible detection of defects. A technique called decision analysis is sometimes helpful in such a determination. This involves an analysis of accept-reject decisions of inspectors and testers, and identifies the point in the process where such decisions are made. Further, the model or part on which such decisions are made is also specified.

Summaries of such results frequently show trends for individual inspectors, especially where inspection planning, visual standards or training is less than adequate. These trends show up in terms of two inspectors servicing the same area and rejecting significantly different amounts of material. Also, decision times (i.e. the time required to make an accept-reject decision) may be significantly different for two inspectors in the same area.

Obviously, the planning engineer must address these differences and provide improved control (and therefore improved costs) by more effectively utilizing the appraisal personnel.

Work Sampling

The technique of work sampling consists of sampling work elements of an individual or group and using probability theory to estimate the total time spent on a given activity. When applied to appraisal personnel, who very often do not have repetitive work elements, it can be used to more effectively structure the work routines. For example, if work sampling determines that 10% of an inspector's time is spent walking from one end of the department to another, then obviously some change in his geographic assignment or work station could be made to minimize such a cost.

Generally, work sampling has been found to be a better tool for measuring indirect labor rather than direct labor, inasmuch as repetitive work elements can be studied by either timestudy or predetermined time standard systems.

Reducing Appraisal Cost Check List

1. Are inspection points located to maximize the return on dollars spent for inspection?
2. Are inspection stations and methods engineered for the most efficient work accomplishment?
3. Could inspection and test operations be economically automated by using special purpose instrumentation, or tape or computer controlled equipment?
4. Could inspection and test record and data reporting functions be more efficiently performed using the computer or other modern data handling devices?
5. Is it possible to control processes sufficiently to prevent production of defectives and eliminate product inspections?
6. Could Statistical Process Control techniques be profitably used?
7. Could tests now being performed by outside laboratories be performed at less cost in-house or vice versa?
8. Are some tasks now being performed by highly paid inspectors or testers which could be performed by lower classification employees?

MEASURING IMPROVEMENT

There are many sources of information on product performance, no one of which usually gives sufficient data to determine whether the customer's needs are being met. It usually takes a combination of sources to get needed data and the optimum combination varies with the product and market. For example, different data sources would be used for a consumer product than for an industrial product. This section contains discussion of many information sources with some of the advantages and disadvantages of each. These sources are:

- Quality costs
- Field failure and repair reports
- Installation phase reporting
- Personal observation by company personnel
- Life testing of company and competitor's finished product
- Market research on customer opinion and user costs
- Data from spare parts sales
- Customer complaints
- Outgoing product audits

Quality Cost Improvement

Do not attempt to measure quality cost improvement solely by looking at total costs or even at ratios. While long term total costs will be reduced with an effective program, short term changes in these costs are not reliable measures of progress. How many product cost improvement programs measure their impact only by comparing overall product costs from one period to another? Most measure success, and each individual's contribution, by measuring and totalling the effect of each individual improvement. In some situations total costs may go up because of increases in wage and material costs, yet the cost improvement program is a success because it prevents a larger rise.

One of the most significant measures of the effect of product failure is the amount of troubleshooting, repair, replacement and liability losses. These charges are normally collected and regularly reported to management as failure costs. They, along with other quality costs, have a direct adverse impact on profits and should be the subject of regular analysis to detect high cost problems and adverse trends. The Pareto analysis is a very valuable tool. As significant as failure costs are, they often do not tell the whole story. Just looking at the amount of these charges does not provide the data necessary for determining problem causes and needed solutions. Although they may be an indication of customer dissatisfaction, there are cases where the costs reported are a small part of the total costs of failure — the cost of the loss of a customer is far more. In such a case, the customer could become quite irritated, but failure cost analysis would not indicate a problem.

Field Trouble Reports

In many companies, field trouble or repair reports are used to report incidents investigated or repaired by repair shops or field engineers. These reports usually contain all information pertinent to the failure such as:

- Customer
- Location
- Customer complaint
- Description of problem
- Repairs necessary
- Estimated repair cost

When properly completed, they can be used to pinpoint products or components of products which are failing and the reasons for failure.

Installation Phase Reporting

Often neglected sources of product quality information are the problems found during the production and commissioning phases of large and complex products. Troubles in this phase are frequently not recorded or reported in a formal way. Companies, manufacturing such products should establish systems for reporting both the costs and causes of them, so corrective action can be taken.

Personal Observation

Management should take every opportunity to see products in operation and to personally investigate major or chronic problems. There is no substitute for seeing a problem first hand. Each person visiting a customer location should be alert to the need for feedback of product performance data to responsible management. Consideration should be given to preparation of a form or guide for this purpose for use by marketing, design engineering, quality assurance or other activities having occasion to make such visits. It is important that these reports be collected and analyzed, along with other feedback data to discover performance problems.

Life Testing

On products where it is feasible, life testing can provide valuable data on product weaknesses. When it is possible to design a test which simulates the product use environment, reliability can be measured and improved and design changes can be proven before incorporation into product going to the customer. Competitor's products can often be subjected to the same testing, resulting in valuable knowledge about the relative strengths and weaknesses of other products in the market. Designing of tests using statistical techniques such as design of experiments, analysis of variance and others is strongly suggested as a means of getting the maximum benefit from the money expended.

Market Research

Market research is a valuable source of information about product performance and customer quality needs. Formal market research studies can take many forms. Some of the most common techniques are:

- Questionnaires to be answered by users or potential users of the product.
- Display of products to a group to obtain preference information.
- Consumer panels and in-use testing of new products to determine the appeal and performance of new products or design changes.
- User or dealer advisory panels which meet regularly to discuss quality and user problems.

Spare Parts Sales

Data from the sale of spare parts is a little used but valuable source of information on product performance. Analysis of this data can identify weak or misapplied parts of the product, and can sometimes help to identify product application problems. Regular analysis of this data should be a part of the quality program wherever such data is available.

Customer Complaints

Action as a result of customer complaints should be:

- Correction of the condition in the product which caused the complaint, i.e., restoration of service, and,
- Correction of the root cause of the problems to prevent recurrence.

The first action, which almost automatically occurs, is often the only action taken on a complaint. A good quality program should require that more be done. Necessary actions beyond restoration of service are:

- Investigation to determine if the incident is isolated or a general problem.
- Analysis of the problem for cause.
- Elimination of cause.
- Regular attention to chronic problems by reporting them and the status of their correction to responsible management.

Outgoing Product Audits

Where appropriate, the quality program should provide for periodic inspection and test of product which has been accepted for shipment to the customer. Such auditing can discover system or product discrepancies far more quickly and at less expense than would be associated with discovery in the field or by the customer.

Reporting Product Performance

Reports summarizing the incidence of field problems should be prepared periodically. A thorough analysis of this information will indicate how well the company is succeeding in satisfying the quality requirements of its customers. It is also an indication of how effective the quality procedures are. It may show where there is a need for adding new controls or for improving the ones that are already in effect. Examples of the kind of information that should be included in the reports are:

- The number of shipments or items that are returned.
- The number of complaints received and the reasons for the complaints.
- A breakdown of field service costs, according to type of reject, cause of reject, and customer.
- Charts showing the cost of returned material, cost of field service, number of customer complaints, and similar information. The information should be so organized that comparisons can be made between the current period and the preceding ones.
- A breakdown of returned material according to the reason for return and according to customer. The analysis should show both the number of units returned and the cost of the returned material.

STRATEGIC PLANNING
GUIDELINE FOR OVER-ALL QUALITY PLAN

One firm's strategic planning process combines an analysis of quality costs with a structured strategic planning process integrated with the overall business plan. Such a plan is developed with the active participation of the general manager of the profit center, his controller and other involved functional managers. Engineering and manufacturing managers are involved since a large portion of the failure costs are their responsibility. The firm's strategic quality planning process is as follows.

1. **Mission**

   State here the unit's quality mission and the principal task of each department responsible for its achievement.

   Specifically define the nature and depth of the services to be performed by the quality organization and identify the recipients of these services.

2. **Quality Function Profit Plan**

   State here briefly, the details of:
   a) **Contributions:** The contributions of the quality function can usually be measured in two areas — quality cost reduction and unit quality image. Include here total cost reductions from section 3-e; the expected status of outgoing quality levels and field performance; and any other planned contributions to overall unit objectives.
   b) **Premises:** State here the major premises upon which the over-all quality plan is based, including a commitment to the budget as stated in section 3-d below.
   c) **Action Planned:** State here the major actions planned to achieve the stated contributions.
   d) **Problems & Strategies:** State here the principal problems that may impede achievement of the stated contributions and the strategies planned for their resolution. Bear in mind that quality program success depends heavily on performance by all functions (Planned strategies should be stated immediately following the associated problem.)

3. **Supporting Cost Data**
a) Quality Cost for Current Products

| | Current Year Forecast | | Plan Year 1 | | Net Increase — $000 |
	$000	% of Sales	$000	% of Sales	Decrease — ($000)
Prevention					
Appraisal					
Failure					
Total COQ					

b) Quality Cost for New Products

| | Current Year Forecast | | Plan Year 1 | | Net Increase — $000 |
	$000	% of Sales	$000	% of Sales	Decrease — ($000)
Prevention					
Appraisal					
Failure					
Total COQ					

c) Total Unit Cost of Quality

| | Current Year Forecast | | Plan Year 1 | | Net Increase — $000 |
	$000	% of Sales	$000	% of Sales	Decrease — ($000)
Prevention					
Appraisal					
Failure					
Total COQ					

d) Quality Department Budget

This pertains to personnel on the quality department/payroll only. Inspection or test personnel working for manufacturing should not be included.

| | Current Year Forecast | | Plan Year 1 | | Net Increase — $000 |
	$000	% of Sales	$000	% of Sales	Decrease — ($000)
Inspection, test and Technician Labor	_____	_____	_____	_____	_____
All other Quality Dept. Labor (Q.E. & Administrative)	_____	_____	_____	_____	_____
Indirect Expenses	_____	_____	_____	_____	_____
Total	_____	_____	_____	_____	_____

e) Cost Reductions

List savings contributed to or originated by the quality department. When the quality department only contributes to a saving, list the partial share that will be allocated to the quality department. Identify planned amounts for each of the following categories.

Category	Amount ($000)		
Labor (any dept.)	_____	Rework	_____
Material	_____	Warranty	_____
Scrap	_____	Total	_____

PROFIT IMPROVEMENT THROUGH
THE TEAM APPROACH

— A CASE STUDY —

A major electrical firm initiated a corporate program to identify, analyze, and reduce quality costs. It was called the Product Integrity Improvement Program — P.I.I. A formal management commitment to improvement of quality and an organized approach to obtaining this improvement has lead to profit improvement at several divisions. This example describes the approach used and the results obtained in one location.

In most industrial environments, the highest segments of total quality costs are found in internal and external failure costs and therefore most organized efforts to reduce costs and improve profits are concentrated in this area. However, it should be stated that by placing greater emphasis in the prevention activity, a significant improvement in quality costs will be realized. The Product Integrity Improvement Program was intended to focus attention on all phases of quality costs and thereby improve the quality, safety, reliability, and environmental effects of products and to reduce the total quality costs.

Establishing and Implementing the Division P.I.I. Program

It was decided to implement the Product Integrity Improvement Program in the example division in order to place greater emphasis on the total quality costs. The primary events that took place to establish and implement this program were as follows:

1. Received top management commitment, support, and involvement.
2. Organized the P.I.I. program in the division.
   a. Assigned the responsibility for the P.I.I. program to a member of the division manager's immediate staff.
   b. Established a P.I.I. council to assist the P.I.I. program manager in determining the overall approach, developing division strategy, and implementing the program. The council members included the division engineering manager, manufacturing manager, controller, and quality control manager.
   c. Conducted a P.I.I. seminar with headquarters quality assurance assistance to introduce the concept to responsible management personnel.
3. Identified the quality costs elements and selected account sources.
4. Collected all the quality costs for the division for the previous twelve months to establish the total quality cost base.
5. Analyzed the division quality cost data and identified the most significant quality cost expenditures. Analysis of the data indicated that internal failure costs were requiring a disproportionate expenditure and should receive the highest priority for action.

As a result of this analysis, total quality costs were found to be:

	Percent Of Sales
Prevention	0.1%
Appraisal	1.5%
Internal Failure	2.3%
External Failure	1.5%
Total	5.4%

Internal failure costs were analyzed to find the high cost contributors with the following results:

Item	Approx. % of Total Internal Failure Cost
Cores	5%
Wire	20%
Coil-Winding — First Assembly	35%
Final Assembly — Test	15%

The coil winding-assembly area was selected since collectively it accounted for the largest portion of the total internal failure cost.

6. Determined basic problems, underlying causes of the problems, and assigned responsibility for corrective action.
   a. Identified three underlying causes:
      (1) Operator winding errors
      (2) Damage to coils in handling
      (3) Design problems
   b. Established a quality improvement working team made up as follows:
      Manufacturing Manager — chairman
      Quality Control Manager
      Manufacturing Engineering — equipment problems
      Engineering — design problems
      General Foreman — operator problems
7. Established quality cost improvement objectives as an integral part of the division's profit plan.
8. Created reporting systems to provide accurate cost visibility and to measure improvement performance.
9. Met weekly to review progress, establish plans, and assign new tasks to be completed.
10. Reviewed monthly total quality costs against the objectives and initiated corrective action where needed.

11. Educated, trained, and emphasized the importance of everyone doing the job right the first time. Employee involvement was most important in attempts to achieve improvement. This was accomplished in a number of ways.
    a. General foreman, quality control supervisor, section foreman meetings at which they
       (1) identified key projects to be worked on
       (2) planned programs for improvement
       (3) reviewed progress
    b. Developed defect charts for each manufacturing section showing objectives and actual costs.
    c. Conducted workplace meetings to establish a "quality-conscious" attitude.
    d. Set-up training programs for certain critical skill, high cost areas.
12. Recognized individuals and/or groups that made significant contributions toward improvement.

The results obtained from this program were significant.

	Costs as a Percent of Sales		
	Previous Year Actual	Current Year Objectives	Current Year Actual
Prevention	0.1	0.1	0.1
Appraisal	1.5	1.3	1.2
Internal failure	2.3	2.0	2.1
Esternal failure	1.5	1.1	1.2
TOTAL	5.4	4.5	4.6

Summary

In summary, the success of a Product Integrity Improvement Program depends on:

1. Top management involvement and support
2. Visible total quality cost data
3. Setting division objectives for improvement and monthly reporting of performance against objectives
4. Organizing for improvement
5. Employee involvement and recognition

The benefits to be gained from a properly implemented P.I.I. Program include:

1. Reduced total quality costs with a corresponding increase in profits.
2. Improved product performance, product integrity, and adherence to schedule.
3. Increased customer acceptance of products and services.
4. Increased repeat sales and new sales from improved product reputation.

FAILURE COST IMPROVEMENT:

General

A major connector manufacturer elected to enter the connector market with a new connector designed to MIL-SPEC. requirements.

The discussion below shows how in four years the product assembly failure cost was reduced from $180K/year to $20K/year.

History

During the early phases of the program, typical startup problems associated with new manufacturing techniques, planning, and training were faced. These items were resolved one-by-one until assembly failure costs were down to about $180,000 in 1971, an amount still considerably above normal for a new connector program.

Three years later, a failure cost plateau of $150,000 per year had been reached, a figure that still was comparatively high. It was not known that a considerable portion of failure dollars originated in the assembly departments. Using the financial data available, failure costs by specific cost center in the assembly departments were identified. (Each cost center is responsible for the assembly of a specific connector type.)

It was seen that two specific cost centers contributed to over 75% of the assembly departments' total failure cost through that period. The one major cost center was the connector assembly cost center and the other center was where bonded assemblies for other connectors are manufactured. This area was also the target for major cost improvements.

From Table 1 it can be seen that, using the first half of the year as a base, holding sales volume constant through the second half of the year, another large dollar failure cost year in the connector area would result. The problem needed to be attacked immediately.

Approach

A review of the prior six months failure history was initiated. All of the discrepancy reports were evaluated, summarized and categorized, and high scrap and rework costs areas were found. (See Chart 1).

It was apparent from this summary that almost 85% of all rejections occurred as the result of contaminated parts due to improperly applied or excessively applied adhesives.

As a result of the excessive cleaning needed to remove the adhesives, an average of 80 connectors per month were scrapped. This alone amounted to almost $20,000 per year.

Cause

Based on these data the causes of the problems were found.

1. Methods employed for adhesives application needed updating for this new connector series.
2. The operators required addtitional training in the application of adhesives.
3. Both operators and inspectors did not understand the complete workmanship standards developed for this program. As a result, the operators were peforming unnecessary rework.
4. Some of the operators were causing a larger percentage of rework and scrap than others.

Corrective Measures

Once the causes were identified, a corrective action team composed of a quality engineer, an industrial engineer and the production supervisor was organized. The production supervisor was appointed to head the team.

This team accomplished the following:

A. The first two months were directed to reviewing manufacturing instructions, revising methods, obtaining new tools and revising the workmanship standards.
B. A new method requiring the application of adhesives through the use of a silk screen technique was introduced.
C. Operators causing a larger percentage of rework and scrap were either retrained or replaced.
D. Finally, the inspectors were retrained in the requirements of the modified workmanship standards.

The costs for these changes were approximately $4,000 in tooling and about $3,000 in labor.

Results

Table 1 compares the results of the first half of year 1 to the second half of year 1. Failure costs in this area decreased dramatically. Note that the failure dollars in the bonded assembly cost center also decreased as a result of application of the same techniques learned in the connector area.

Table 1 also compares the results of Year 1 to Year 2. The results have yielded a net savings in failure cost of almost $80K for Year 2 in the connector area despite increased sales volume. There was also, a $34K savings in the bonding area.

Summary

By using the tools available, a problem was identified, its cause found and corrective action initiated to prevent recurrence. This resulted in a net savings equivalent to a sales increase of over $350,000 on these products! This was accomplished by recognizing that small pieces of a larger problem can more easily be digested and resolved one at a time.

Examples

TABLE 1

FAILURE COSTS BY COST CENTER

	CC: 2441 (BONDING) ($ 000)	CC: 2450 (CONNECTOR ASSEMBLY) ($ 000)
FIRST HALF YEAR 1	57.6	67.0
SECOND HALF YEAR 1	17.7	34.0
TOTAL YEAR 1	75.3	101.0
TOTAL YEAR 2	41.2	22.0
NET SAVINGS	34.1	79.0

CHART 1

REJECTION CAUSES

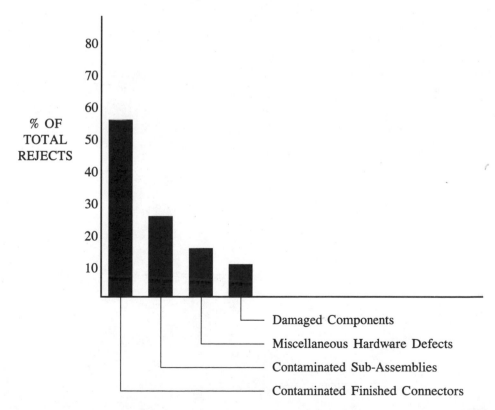

Damaged Components

Miscellaneous Hardware Defects

Contaminated Sub-Assemblies

Contaminated Finished Connectors

QUALITY COSTS — GENERAL DESCRIPTION

Prevention Costs — The costs of all activities specifically designed to prevent defects in deliverable products or service. Includes activities prior to and during product or service development, purchasing, operations planning and execution, operations support, and post delivery service. Examples include development progress reviews, supplier capability surveys, process capability evaluations, quality education and training. Includes labor and fringe benefit costs, as well as expenses and depreciation.

Appraisal Costs — The costs associated with measuring, evaluating or auditing products or services to assure conformance to quality standards and performance requirements. These include the inspection, test or audit of purchased materials, manufacturing or process operations, operations support documentation and materials, and installation or field trials. Includes labor and fringe benefit costs, as well as expenses and depreciation.

Failure Costs — The costs required to evaluate and either correct or replace products or services not conforming to requirements or customer/user needs. This includes purchased materials, and associated product or service design and support materials because they failed to meet requirements or customer/user needs. Includes both material and labor costs, with fringe benefits.

Internal Failure Costs — These costs occur prior to completion or shipment of the product, or furnishing of a service.

External Failure Costs — These costs occur after shipment of the product, and during or after furnishing of a service.

BIBLIOGRAPHY
PUBLICATIONS AND PAPERS RELATING TO
QUALITY COSTS CONCEPTS AND IMPROVEMENT

Adamek, Kenneth, C., "Automated Collective Analysis of Scrap and Rework", *ASQC 33rd ATC*, Houston, May 1979, pp. 190-199

Aerospace Industries Association, "Quality Resources Study", 1970, QAC PROJECT 71.7

Agnone, A.M.; Brewer, C.C., Caine, R.V., Aerospace Electronics Systems Department, General Electric Co., Utica, NY, "Quality Cost Measurement and Control", *27th AQC*, Cleveland, 1973

Akerlung, O.O.; Condon, J.; Kidwell, J.L.; Rosenthal, A.B. "Money — 1: A Measure of Value" *Quality Progress*, Sep 75, pp. 24-25

Albrecht, Glenn, R., "Scrap Cost Analysis in a Mass Production Industry", *21st AQC*, May 67

Alford, E., "Quality Costs — Where to Start? Part I" *Quality*, Aug 79, pp. 36-37

Alford, E., "Quality Costs — Where to Start? Part II" *Quality*, Sep 79, pp. 70-71

Alford, E., "Quality Costs — Where to Start? Part III" *Quality*, Oct 79, pp. 40-42

Allen, Paul, "Quality Control Budget Methods", *9th ATC*, New York, 1955, pp. 97-103

Allen, Paul E., "Evaluating Inspection Costs", *21st AQC* May 67

Armstrong, Willis C., "Quality and the International Economic Scene", *Quality Progress*, Jul 73, p. 17

ASQC Aircraft-Missile Division, "Quality Cost Analysis Implementation Handbook", Sep 1964

ASQC Aircraft Missile Division, "Some Models of Quality Cost Analysis for Industry", June 1964

ASQC Quality Costs Committee, *Quality Costs What and How*, 1974, 54 pages

ASQC Quality Costs Committee, *Guide For Reducing Quality Costs*, 1977, 46 pages

ASQC Quality Costs Committee, *Principles of Quality Costs*, 1986, 71 pages

ASQC Quality Costs Committee, *Quality Costs: Ideas and Applications*, 1984, 526 pages

Armstrong, Francis, "Reliability and Cost as Factors in Standards Enforcement", *26th ATC*, Washington, 1972

Aubrey, Charles A.; Zimbler, Debra A., "A Banking Quality Cost Model, Its Uses and Results", *36th AQC*, Detroit 1982

Aubrey, Charles A. and Zimbler, Debra A., "The Banking Industry: Quality Costs and Improvement", *Quality Progress*, Dec 83, pp. 16-19

Aubrey, J.; Dintino, J., "A Look at the Real Cost of Procurement", *Quality*, May 76, pp. 20-23

Ball, A.M., "Quality Cost and Management", *21st ATC* May 67

Baker, K. R., "Two Cost Models for Economic Design of An X Bar Chart", 22nd *Industrial Engineering Proceedings*, 1970, pp. 337. FAM

Baker, W. R., "The Impact of Quality on Cost", *Quality Progress*, Nov 69

Barker, E.M., "Counting Costs: Another Approach to Supplier Ratings", *Quality Progress*, Nov 84

Barrabee, James M.; "The Development of a Scrap Cost Program" *Industrial Quality Control*, Jan 65

Bather, J. A., "Control Charts and Minimization of Costs", Ser. B. 25, pp 49-80, 1963, FAM

Baugher, John, "Profitable Quality Control", *Production Magazine*, Sep 68

Bayer, Harmon, S., "Quality Control Programs Should be Cost Reduction Programs", *14th ATC*, May 1960

Bhuyan, Samar, K., "Cost of Quality as a Customer Perception" *36th AQC*, Detroit, May 82

Bicking, Charles A., "Cost and Value Aspects of Quality Control", *Industrial Quality Control*, Dec 67

Blanchard, B.S., "Cost Effectiveness Analysis — A Case Study Approach", *23rd ATC*, Los Angeles, May 1969

Blank, L.; Solorzano, J., "Using Quality Costs Analysis for Management Improvement", *Industrial Engineering*, Feb 78, pp. 46-51

Boerckel, Albert, "The Formula for Survival — Optimum Quality at Optimum Cost", *1973 Annual Reliability and Maintainability Symposium*, IEEE Catalog 73 CHO714-6P

Booth, C. E., "Computer Simulation of Life Cycle Cost Elements", *23rd ATC*, Los Angeles, 1969

Booth, William E., "Financial Reporting of Quality Performance", *Quality Progress*, Feb 77, pp. 14-15

Booth, B., "Charge Back-Accountability Systems Reduce Quality Costs to 2.1% of Annual Sales", *Quality Progress*, 1971

Boudreault, Arthur L., "Quality Control, A Savings Center", *Quality*, Sep 77, pp. 20-21

Blanchard, Ben S., "Cost Effectiveness Analysis — A Case Study Approach", *23rd ATC* May, 69

Bradshaw, C.W., "Application of Economic Principles to Quality", *38th ATC*, Chicago, 1984

Brainard, E.H., "Quality Measurement and Reporting as Related to Management Cybernetics, *28th ATC*, May 74 pp. 208-219

Bramblett, J.; Sadosky, T.; Wadsworth, H.; "Control Charts Based on Cost for Use in Service Industries", *Administrative Applications Division Yearbook*, 1974

Branin, George, "Buy Quality with a Live-in Rep", *Quality*, Jan 76, pp. 14-16

Brewer, C.W., "Quality Costs — View and Preview", *34th ATC*, Atlanta, May 1980

Brewer, Clyde W., "Zero Based Profit Assurance", *Quality Progress*, Jan 78, pp 25-27

Breeze, J. D.; Farrell, J. R., "Quality Costs Can be Sold — Part II", *35th AQC*, 1981

Brisac, A.; Oistrach, G.; Yanez, O., "Quality Cost Data in 3 Spanish Automotive Companies", *Quality*, No. 4, 1971 pp. 99-104

Brown, F. X., "Quality Cost and Profit Performance", *32nd ATC*, Chicago, May 1978

Brown, F. X., "How to Win Friends and Influence Profits", *35th AQC*, 1981

Brown, F. X., "Quality Costs and Strategic Planning", *34th ATC*, Atlanta, May 1980

Brown, F. X., "The Quality Accounting Relationship", Fall Workshop, Akron-Canton Section, Nov 5, 1976

Brown, T.H., "Market Research Sets QC Targets", *9th ATC*, New York, 1955, pp 653-659

Brumbaugh, Martin, "QC Saves", *Quality Progress*, Jun 74, p 9

Burbridge, H. K., "Better Value with Design to Life Cycle Costs", *Quality*, Dec 77., pp. 14-17

Burchfield, P.B. and Thorton, P. A., "Quality Costing Procedures Reduce Cable Losses", *Wire Technology*, Jan 1982

Burns, V. P., "Warranty Prediction: Putting a $ on Poor Quality", *Quality Progress*, Dec 70, p. 28

Cabral, W. O., "Quality Cost Myopia", *37th AQC*, Boston, May 1983

Calahan, C.C., "Reporting Analysis and Control of Costs in a Multifactory Company", *20th ATC*, May 1966, New York

Campanella, Jack, "The Fairchild Republic Company Quality Cost Program", *33rd ATC*, Houston, May 79, pp 584-593

Campanella, Jack, "A Simplified Approach to the Use of Costs Related to Quality", *13th All Day Conference*, Long Island Section, Apr 75, pp. 15-20

Campanella, Jack; Corcoran, Frank J., "Principles of Quality Costs — II", *36th AQC*, May 82

Campanella, Jack; Corcoran, Frank J., "Principles of Quality Costs" *Quality Progress*, Apr 83, pp. 16-22

Caplan, Frank, "Managing Success Through the Quality System", *38th AQC*, Chicago, 1984

Cartin, R. J., "Quality Capability at Less Cost" *Industrial Quality Control*, Feb 62, pp. 14-16

Cawsey, R. A., "A Business Performance Measure of Quality Management", *30th ATC*, Toronto, May 76, pp. 139-143

Bibliography

Cerzosimo, R.R., "Honeywell's Cost Effective Defect Control Through Quality Information Systems", *26th ATC* Washington, May 1972

Chalmers, Allis, "When Does a Quality System Provide Optimum Contributions", *Quality Mgmnt and Engrg*, Feb 73

Champernowne, P. G., "The Economics of Sequential Sampling Procedures for Defectives", *Applied Statistics* 2, 1953, pp. 118-130

Chateauneuf, Robert, "Modern QC Pays Off in Woodwork", *Industrial Quality Control*, Sep 60, pp 19-25

Churchill, G. W., "Minimizing the Cost of Lot Sampling Through Computer Solution of Cost-Probability Equations" *22nd ATC*, May 68

Condon, J. E.; Kidwell, J. L., Akerlund, O. O., "Quality Cost Panel", *29th ATC*, San Diego, May 75

Corcoran, Frank J.,; Campanella, Jack, "Principles of Quality Costs — I", *36th AQC*, Detroit, May 82

Corcoran, Frank J., "Quality Costs Principles — A Preview", *34th ATC*, Atlanta, May 1980

Cotton, F.E., "Profit Oriented Quality Engineering", *1965 ATC*, Los Angeles, pp. 629-638

Cound, D.M., "Quality System Analysis — Key to Recurring Cost Reduction", *1965 ATC*, Los Angeles, pp. 109-115

Crosby, P., "Cost of Quality — Elements by Discipline", *The Quality College*, Orlando, FL, October 1982

Crosby, P., *Cutting the Cost of Quality*, Hitchcock Publishing Co., FAM

Crosby, P., "Don't Be Defensive about Quality Costs", *Quality Progress*, Apr 83, pp. 38-39

Davies, O.L., "Some Statistical Aspects of the Economics of Analytical Testing", *Technometrics* 1, 1959, pp. 49-61

Dawes, E. W., "Improving Quality/Productivity in Plastic Molding", *Quality Progress*, Nov 73, pp. 22-26

Dawes, E. W., "Quality Costs — A Tool for Improving Organization", *28th Northeast Conference*, Albany, 1974

Dawes, E. W., "Optimizing Attribute Sampling Costs — A Case Study", *27th ATC*, May 73

Dawes, E. W., "Is Your Quality Cost Dollar Really Effective?" *27th Northeast Conference*, Boston, Oct 73

Dawes, E. W., "Reducing Appraisal Costs", *32nd ATC*, Chicago, May 1978

Dawes, E. W., "Quality Costs — A Place on the Shop Floor", *30th ATC*, Toronto, 1976, pp. 123-128

Dawes, E. W., "Quality Costs — A Tool for Improving Profits", *Quality Progress*, Sep 75, pp. 12-13

Dauton, J. D., "Fine Tuning Inspection for Minimum Costs", *Quality*, Nov 77, pp. 46-49

Dr. Ing. Allessandro Codeca de Ferrara, "Inspection and Quality Costs", *Proceedings VII EOQC Conferenie*, pp 101-108

Dean, T. J., "A Successful Quality Cost Program", *28th Northeast Conference*, Albany, Oct 74

Demetriou, J., "Quality Costs — Pay" *36th AQC*, May 82

Demetriou, J., "Cost of Quality System — A Management Tool" *37th AQC*, Boston, May 83

Dobbins, R. K., "Cost Effectiveness of Corrective Action", *1972 Philadelphia Section Annual Symposium*

Dobbins, R. K., "Extending Effectiveness of Quality Cost Programs", *32nd ATC*, Chicago, May 1978

Dobbins, R. K., "Designing an Effective Procurement Rating System", *34th ATC*, Atlanta, May 1980

Dobbins, R. K., "Quality Cost Analysis — Quality Assurance vs Accounting", *1973 Philadelphia Section Annual Symposium*

Dobbins, R. K., "Total Quality Cost Analysis — Quality Cost Management for Profit", *1971 Philadelphia Section Annual Symposium*

Dobbins, R. K., "Quality Cost Trend Analysis and Corrective Action", *26th Annual Conference on QC and Statistics in Industry*, Rutgers, Sep 74

Dobbins, R. K., "Quality Costs — A Place for Decision Making and Corrective Action", *30th ATC*, Toronto, 1976, pp. 112-115

Dobbins, R. K., "Your Quality Posture — A Profit/Survival Challenge", *35th AQC*, 1981

Dobbins, R., "Quality is Business — Which Management Commitment?", *37th AQC*, May 83

Duncan, A. J. and Bowen, G. L., "Boosting Product Qualtiy for Profit Improvement", *Manufacturing Engineering*, Apr 84, pp. 106-108

Duke, E.M., "Do You Spell Relief — Quality?" *35th ATC*, San Francisco, May 1981

Dunn, T. H., "Quality Control Costing", *The Quality Engineer*, vol. 33, no. 6

Durbin, I. P., "Pricing Policies Contingent on Observed Product Quality", *Technometrics 8*, 1966, pp. 123-124

Dwyer, M. J., "Cost Effective Quality", *24th ATC*, 70

Ekvall, D.N., "Measuring the Profitability of QC Effectiveness", *26th ATC*, Washington, May 1972

Elgabry, A.C., "Integrated Quality Control Cost", *30th ATC*, Toronto, 1976, pp. 144-153

Ennerson, F., "How Many Dollars are There in Incoming Inspection Costs?", *14th ATC*, May 60

Enrick, N. L., "Document Your Quality Achievements", *Quality Management and Engineering*, Oct 75, pp. 22-23

Enters, J. H., "Design and Quality Costs, Quality of Design and Design of Quality", *Proceedings VII EOQC* Conferentie

Esterby, L.J., "Quality Cost Analysis: A Productivity Measure", *35th AQC*, 1981

Esterby, L.J., "Measuring Quality Costs by Work Sampling", *36th AQC*, May 1982

Fiegenbaum, A. V., Chapter 5, pp 83-106, *Total Quality Control*, McGraw-Hill, 1961, FAM

Fiegenbaum, A. V., "Some Next Steps in Quality Control:, *Industrial Quality Control*, Sep 62, pp. 5-11

Field, D. L., "Thoughts on the Economics of Quality", *Industrial Quality Control*, Oct 66

Filer, R. J.; Eiswerth, L.R., "Quality Control and Associated Costs", *Management Accounting 48*, 1966 pp. 37-44

Filer, J.M., "Quality Cost Reporting", *23rd Western Regional Conference*, 1976

Freeman, H. L., "How to Put Quality Costs to Work", *12th Metropolitan Section All Day Conference*, Sep 60

Frisinger, A.H.I., "Quality Costs and Quality Control Evaluation in Electromechanical Industry", *Proceedings VII EOQC Conference*

Fruehwirth, M.Z., "PSQL — An Economic Criterion for Minimizing Overall Inspection and Repair Cost", *28th ATC*, May 74, pp. 330-337

Funk, B. I., "Costs of Reliability", *Industrial Quality Contron*, Sep 60, pp. 31-33

Gadzinski, C., "Control of Quality Costs in Mfg", *The Manufacturing Man and His Job*, AMA, 1966

Galbraith, Bruce; Berger, Richard, "Dollar Value Sampling Plans", *Quality Assurance*, Apr 68, pp. 30-33

Garvin, D.A., "Quality on the Line", *Harvard Business Review*, Sep-Oct 1983, pp. 65-74

Georgis, G. S., "How Much Does Poor Quality Cost", *Management Review*, May 73

Gilmore, H., "Product Conformance Cost", *Quality Progress*, Jun 74, pp. 16-19

Gilmore, H., "Consumer Product QC Cost Revisited", *Quality Progress*, Apr 83, pp. 28-32

Goeller, W. D., "The Cost of Software Quality Assurance", *35th AQC*, 1981

Goeller, W. D., "On the Road to Quality Savings", *39th AQC*, 1985

Goetz, V. J., "Developing a Cost Effectiveness Program — How to Start", *33rd ATC*, Houston, May 79, pp. 156-160

Gonet, J. J., "Improving the Management of Quality Cost", *22nd ATC*, May 68

Gottfried, P., "A Preliminary Cost/Probability Model for a Multi-Satellite System", *1964 ATC*, Buffalo, pp. 31-43

Bibliography

Grant and Bell, "Quality Costs", *Basic Accounting and Cost Accounting*, McGraw-Hill, 1956, pp. 386-396

Grant and Levenworth, "Some Economic Aspects of Quality Decisions", *Statistical Quality Control*, McGraw-Hill, Fourth Edition, pp. 593-610

Grau, D, "Quality, Inexpensive if a Way of Life", *Quality Progress*, Feb 72, p. 20

Grenier, R, "Recover Those Defective Material Costs", *Quality Management and Engineering*, Feb 75, pp. 26-27

Grimm, A. F., "Quality Costs — Where Are They in the Accounting Process", *28th ATC*, May 74, pp. 190-200

Groocock, J. M., "Quality Cost Reporting", *The Cost of Quality*, Pitman Publishing, First Edition, London, pp. 8-29

Groocock, J. M., "A Decade of Quality in a European Multinational", *31st ATC*, Philadelphia

Gryna, F. M., "User Quality Costs", *Quality Progress*, Nov 72 pp 18-21

Gryna, F. M., "Quality Costs — User vs Manufacturer", *Quality Progress*, Jun 77, pp. 10-13

Gryna, F. M., "Quality Costs — What Does Management Expect?", *32nd ATC*, Chicago, May 1978

Gryna, F., "Marketing Research and Product Quality" *37th AQC*, Boston, May 83

Guenther, W. C., "On the Determination of Single Sampling Attribute Plans Based Upon a Linear Cost Model and a Prior Distribution", *Technometrics* 13, 1971, pp. 483-498

Gunneson, A. O., "How to Effectively Implement a Quality Cost System", *35th ATC*, 1981

Hagan, J. T., "The Cost of Quality", *A Management Role for Quality Control*, Chapter 18, 1968, The American Management Association

Hagan, J. T., "Quality Costs at Work", *27th ATC*, 1973

Hagan, J. T., "Quality Costs — Detailed Definitions", *Akron/Canton Fall Workshop*, Nov 5, 1976

Hagan, J. T., "After the Commitment, Then What?", *35th AQC*, 1981

Hagan, J. T., "Quality Costs II", *39th AQC*, 1985

Hains, R. W., "Economics of Quality", *23rd ATC*, Los Angeles, May 1969

Hald, A, "The Compound Hypergeometric Distribution and a System for Single Sampling Inspection Plans Based on Prior Distributions and Costs", *Technometrics* 2, 1960, pp. 275-340

Hald, A., "Efficiency of Sampling Inspection Plans for Attributes", *Bulletin of the International Statistics Institute*, 34, pp 681-697, 1964

Hamaker, H. C., "Economic Principles in Industrial Sampling Problems", *Bulletin of the International Statistics Institute* 33, pp. 105-122

Hansel, J. L., "Corrective Action and Pareto — The Perfect Marriage", *33rd ATC*, Houston, May 1979

Hansen, B.L., "Quality Costs", *Quality Control — Theory and Applications*, Chapter 3, pp. 45-47, 1963

Hamburg, M., "Bayesian Decision Theory and Statistical Quality Control", *15th ATC*, May 61

Harrington, H. J., "The Shadow Over the Quality Cost Curves", IBM Technical Report TR02.588, Sep 24, 1973, IBM General Products Division

Harrington, H. J., "Prevention's Impact on Quality Cost", IBM Technical Report TR02.1096, Mar 1, 1984, IBM General Products Division

Harrington, H. J., "The Productivity and Quality Connection", IBM Technical Report TR02.1033, May 20, 1983, IBM General Products Division

Harrington, H. J., "Productivity and Quality: A Natural Marriage for Profit", IBM Technical Report TR02.911, Jan 15, 1981, IBM General Products Division

Harrington, H. J., "Quality Costs — A Key to Productivity", *35th AQC*, 1981

Harrington, H. J., "Quality Costs — The Whole and its Parts", *Quality*, May 76, pp. 34-35

Harris, E. A., "Quality Costs as a Guide to Management and Design of Automobile Components", *ICQC Proceedings*. Tokyo, 1969, pp. 273-276

Harvey, J.E., "Procurement Problems Relevant to Quality Control", *15th Annual Metropolitan Section Conference*, Sep 63

Heady, B. O., "Stylizing Incoming Inspection", *Quality Progress*, Mar 70, p. 28

Hendrickson, R.J., "Let's Forget About Quality — Let's Go For Profit", *Quality Management and Engineering*, Mar 71

Hickey, W. J., "An $X00,000 Saving by Sampling Paperwork", *Industrial Quality Control*, Jun 64

Hird, J. F., "Your Quality Improvement Program" *Quality Assurance*, Nov. 62, pp 32-36

Hird, J. F., "Integrated Quality Cost Control", *ICQC Proceedings*, Tokyo, 1969, pp. 269-271

Hitzelberger, "Having $ Problems", *Quality Assurance,* Apr 64

Hocheiser, Seymour, Rhodes, "Quality Costs for Environmental Monitoring Systems", *31st ATC*, Philadelphia, pp 328-338

Hoekstra, C. D., "Quality Costs as a Basis for Efficient Quality Control", *10th Western Regional Conference*, ASQC, 1963

Holguin, R., "Do You Know What Cost Reductions Can Do For You?", *Quality Progress*, Jan 68, p. 22

Hutter, R.G., "Inspection Manpower Planning", *Industrial Quality Control*, Apr 66

Ireson, W. G., "Cost Data — Collection and Use", *1966 Proceedings on Reliability and Quality Control*, Jan 66

Ireson, W. G., "Cost Control of Quality And Reliability", *11th Aircraft and Missile Division Conference*, 1961 Los Angeles

Ireson, W. G., "The Control and Optimization of Quality Costs", *19th ATC*, May 65

Ireson, W. G., "Use of Quality Cost Information in Planning and Managing Quality Assurance Programs", *21st ATC*

Irving, R.R., "QC Payoff Attracts Top Management", *Iron Age*, Aug 20, 79, pp. 64-65

Jones, H.C., "Selecting Consumer's Risk to Minimize Cost", *1966 ATC*, Baltimore, pp. 423-431

Jorgensen, J., "Utilizing Quality Cost Information", *Proceedings VII ECQC Conference*, 1963, pp 49-57

Judelson, P. J., "Estimating Quality Control Engineering Costs for Proposals", *Industrial Quality Control*, Nov 67

Juran and Gryna, *Quality Planning and Analysis*, 1970, Chapters 4 and 5

Juran, J.M., "Whose Quality Costs", *Industrial Quality Control*, Aug 65

Juran, J.M., "Quality Cost Analysis", *Management of Quality*, pp. M1-M23

Juran, J.M., "The Quality Profit Relationship", *30th ATC*, Toronto, 1976, pp 18-29

Juran and Lundvac, "Quality Costs", *Quality Control Handbook*, 3rd Edition, McGraw-Hill, Chapters 4-5

Kahn, H. R., "Quality Costs — Critical Factor in the Reliability Business", *21st ATC*, ASQC, May 67

Kao, EPC 1972, "Economic Screening of a Continuously Manufactured Product", *Technometrics* 14, pp 653-661

Karpouzis, P. D., "A Quality Effort Pays Off", *Quality Progress*, Nov 68

Kennedy, W.J., "A Cost Determined Quality Control Plan for Adjustable Processes", *24th ATC*, Pittsburgh, May 1970

Kidwell, J. L., "3 Step Plan to Quality Profitability", *Quality Management and Engineering*, Nov 71

Kivendo, K., "Quality Costs — A Place for the Quality Control Organization", *30th ATC*, Toronto, 1976, pp 134-148

Kolacek, O. G., "Quality Costs — A Place for Financial Impact", *30th ATC*, Toronto, 1976, pp. 129-133

Kofoed, C. A., "Applied Methods and Techniques for Control of Quality Costs", *29th ATC*, 1966, pp. 274-280

Kohl, William F., "Hitting Quality Costs Where They Live", *Management Review*, Jul 72, pp. 3-10

Koga, Y., "Activities for Reduction of User's Costs", *24th ATC*, Pittsburgh, May 1970

Bibliography

Kroeger, R. C., "Quality Costs — A New Perspective", *33rd ATC*, Houston, May 79, pp. 575-583

Kuhn, J.P., "Establishing An Effective Quality Information Feedback System", *25th ATC*, Chicago, 1971

Kuzmin, W. R., "Quality Planning for Profit", *10th Western Regional Conference*, ASQC, Feb 63

Lally, F.A., "Quality — Whose Responsibility?", *26th ATC*, Washington, May 1972

Ladue, H. J., "An Effective Management Tool", *Industrial Quality Control*, Dec 65

Lamb, C. P., "Overcoming Resistance and the Quality Stigma", *Quality Progress*, May 74, pp. 12-15

Latherow, J., "Implementation of the Quality Data Systems at McDonnell Aircraft", *34th ATC*, Atlanta, 1980

Lancaster, E.J., "RESAQLXE$C", *Quality Assurance*, May 63, p. 31

Lancaster, E. J.; Beodembemder, "A Critique of QA Activity in Air Force Ballistic Missile Programs — Parts 1, 2, 3", *Industrial Quality Control*, Jan, Feb, Mar 1962

Latzko, W. J., "Quality Productivity Measures — Participation Management", *35th ATC*, San Francisco, May 81

Latzko, W. J., "Reducing Clerical Quality Costs", *28th ATC*, May 74, pp. 185-189

Latzko, W. J., "Quality Productivity Measures — Participative Management", *35th AQC*, 1981

Latzko, W. J., "Minimizing the Cost of Inspection", *36th AQC*, Detroit, 1982

Lavery, J. RE., "Systems and Data Analysis of Quality Costs", *27th Northeast Regional Conference*, ASQC, Boston, 73T

Lebre, R.G., "Quality Costs — Fresh Interest in a Profit Builder", *Quality Assurance*, Jan 66, pp. 26-28

Lee, D.D., "Minimized Cost Sampling Techniques", *35th ATC*, San Francisco, May 81

Lehman, H., "Cost Effectiveness Applied to Product Assurance", *Annals of Reliability and Maintainability*

Leibert, F. P., "Guidelines on the Gathering and Implementation of QC", *The Quality Engineer*, Vol 32, no 2

Lesser, W. H., "Cost of Quality", *1953 ATC*, Philadelphia, pp. 551-559

Lester, R.H., "The Hidden Sales Force", *Quality*, Nov 78, p. 18

Liebman, M.E., "A Management Quality Cost Reporting System", *23rd ATC*, Los Angeles, May 69

Liebesman, B. S., "Selection of MIL STD 105D Plans Based on Cost", *35th AQC*, 1981

Lock, L. G., "Bayesian Statistics", *Industrial Quality Control*, Apr 64

Lundvall, D. M., "Unmasking the Hidden Costs of Getting Quality", *Mill and Factory*, Sep 66

Lundvall, D. M., "Control Potential and Cost Measurement:, *Industrial Quality Control*, Vol 14, no 4, pp. 14-20

Malloy and Kohl, "When Does a Quality System Provide Optimum Profit Contribution?", *Quality Management and Engineering*, Feb 73

Mandel, B. J., "Quality Costing Systems", *Quality Progress*, Dec 72

Mandleson, J, "Sampling Plans for Destructive or Expensive Testing", *Industrial Quality Control*, Mar 67

Marks, R.P., "Micro-Computer Applications for Quality", *38th AQC*, Chicago, 1984

Martin, C.A., "Determination of an Optimum Acceptance Plan Based on Cost", *1962 ATC*, Cincinnati, pp. 143-150

Martin, Cyrus, A., "Optimum Destructive Sampling Based Upon Cost", *17th ATC*, May 63

Martin, Cyrus A., "The Cost Breakeven Point in Attribute Sampling", *Industrial Quality Control*, Sep 64

Masser, W. J., "The Quality Manager and Quality Costs:, *Industrial Quality Control*, Oct 57, pp. 5-8

Mayben, J. E., "Computer Isolation of Significant Quality Costs", *35th AQC*, 1981

Mayben, J. E., "Assurance of Availability and Life Cycle Costs", *36th AQC*, Detroit, 1982

McAllister, J. F., "Realistic Quality Costs", *28th Northeast Regional Conference*, Albany, 1974

McKechnie, J. C., "Minimum Cost Inspection Levels", *Quality Assurance*, Jul 64, p. 25

McRobb, R. M., "Control the Quality of Specifications", *Quality Management and Engineering*, May 75, pp. 18-20

Mertz, O.R., "Quality's Role in ROI", *Quality Progress*, Oct, 77, pp. 14-18

Meske, A., "A Management Standard for Economic Inspection", *Quality*, Jan 76, pp. 28-30

Metsher, W. E., "Measuring Quality Department Effectiveness", *Industrial Quality Control*, Feb 73

Miller, R. H., "Product Evaluation Produces Lower Costs", *23rd ATC*, May 69

Millhouse, R. C., "Total Quality Costs" *23rd ATC*, May 69

Mitchell, M., "Setting Up a Quality System in a Small Business", *34th ATC*, May 1980

Mills, J. E., "Timely Corrective Action Pays", *33rd ATC*, 1979

Montgomery, D.C.; Mance, J. F.; Heikes, R G, "An Economic Model the Fraction Defective with Multiple Assignable Causes", *28th ATC*, May 74

Moore, W.M., "The Philosophy and Usefullness of Quality Costs", *32nd ATC*, Chicago, May 78

Moore, W. N., "Reducing Quality Costs", *26th ATC*, May 72

Moseley, R. Z., "Component Failure Cost", *Quality Progress*, Jan 1980

Mottley and Enrick, "Quality Cost System for the Small Supplier", *Quality Management and Engineering*, Feb 73

Mottley, H. E., "Quality Costs in Taiwan", *Quality Progress*, Sep 72, p 17

Mundel, A., "Quality Cost Breakthroughs in US Production", *37th AQC*, Boston, May 83

Murthy, V., "Quality Costs — A Management Tool", *37th AQC*, Boston, May 83

Murray, T., W., "Quality and Reliability Costs", *Quality Engineer* 31, p. 4

Nambo, H., "Quality Cost System in Nippon Kayaku Co.", *1966 ATC*, New York, pp. 381-386

National Council for Quality and Reliability, "Quality Costs", Great Britain, Nov 70

Nelson, R. H., "Design Internal Competition into Cost Reduction and Control", *13th Annual Metropolitan Section Conference*, Sep 61

Nickel, K. W., "Quality Costs — A Method for Rating Vendors", *16th ATC*, May 62

Nixon, F., "Organization, Man and Reliability", *Industrial Quality Control*, Aug 62, pp. 15-21

Norton, L. N., "Quality is Profit", *Quality Assurance*, Jun 76, pp. 43-47

Norton, L. N.; Carter, T. M., "Economic Importance of Quality and Reliability", *Quality* 1965, pp. 99-104

Noz, W.; Redding, B.; Ware, P., "The Quality Manager's Job: Optimize Costs", *37th AQC*, Boston, May 83

O'Callaghan, M., "Predominant Quality Cost Problems as they Exist in the American Industry", *19th ATC*, May 65

Oak, A.D., "Cost Approach to SQC Charts", *Quality Progress*, Sep 74, pp. 28-29

Ortwein, W. J., "Increased Profits Through Company-Wide Commitment", *39th AQC*, 1985

Ortwein, W. J., "Study Cost and Improve Productivity", *36th AQC*, May 82

Owen, G. E., "Determining Quality Costs", *Industrial Quality Control*, Aug 65

Oyrzanowski, B., "Technicians vs Economists in Quality Control", *EOQC Journal*, Summer 74

Oyrzanowski, B. and Skrzypczak, J., "Quality Costs in a Branch", *21st EOQC Conference*, vol 1, pp 427-435

Pattom, J. D., "Deciding When to Service or Replacc Equipment", *31st ATC*, pp. 20-27

Peterson, C., "Selecting a Product Quality Level", *Quality Engineering*, Aug 73, p. 23

Pennell, A. B., "Value Analysis and Quality Control", *16th ATC*, May 62

Pierce, R. J.; Beame, R. E., "A Matter of Management — Quality Costs for Missile and Space Products", *19th ATC*, May 76

Bibliography

Pippitt, R. G., "More Than Cost Reduction", *Quality Progress*, Jun 69, pp. 18-20

Pitt, H., "Pareto Revisited", *Quality Progress*, May 74, pp. 29-30

Pollard, R. L., "Management Budget Control: Quality Labor Standards", *31st ATC*, pp. 240-246

Purcell, W. E., "Quality Cost Control", *Industrial Quality Control*, May 62

Purcell, W. E., "Quality Cost Control" *15th ATC*, May 61

Puanzagl, J., "Sampling Procedure Based on Prior Distribution and Costs", *Technometrics* 5, 1963, pp 47-61

Puanzagl, J.; Schuler, W., "The Efficiency of Sequential Sampling Plans Based on Prior Distribution and Costs", *Technometrics* 12, 1970, pp. 299-312

Pyzdek, T., "Impact of Quality Cost Reduction on Profits", *Quality Progress*, Nov 76, pp. 14-15

"Quality Cost Survey", *Quality*, Jun 77

"The Cost of Quality", *Quality Assurance*, Jul 63

"An Anatomy of a Financial Report", *Quality Management and Engineering*, Feb 75, pp. 18-2-, Mar 75, pp. 26-27, Apr 75, pp. 18-19

"Quality Costs: The Real Measurement of Performance", *Qualtiy Management and Engineering*, Jan 75, pp. 26-29

Raymond, A. S.; Wambach, G. W., "The Optimum Sampling Plan", *31st ATC*, pp. 574-578

Reames, J. P., "Profit Improvement Through Scrap Reduction", *38th AQC*, Chicago, 1984

Reynolds, R. G., "Life Cycle Costing — Achieving the Proper Balance", *31st ATC*, pp. 564-567

Reynolds, F. A., "Starting Improved Control", *Industrial Quality Control*, Vol 22, no. 78, pp. 336-340

Rhodes, R. C., "Implementing a Quality Cost System", *Quality Progress*, Feb 72

Rhodes, R. D.; Hochheiser, S., "Quality Cost Concepts for Environmental Monitoring Systems", *30th ATC*

Richardson, E. L.; Bennett, E. C., "Quality Cost Control Trial Program", *10th Annual Western Regional Conference*, ASQC, Feb 63

Rogers, C. B., "Uncovering the Hidden Costs of Defective Material", *26th ATC*, May 72

Rosenzweig, G., "Cost of Quality in the Service Industries", *32nd ATC*, Chicago, May 78

Rosenthal, A. B., "Designer's Role in Meeting Societal Quality Demands", *33rd ATC*, May 79, pp. 175-180

Rossie, J. R., "Cutting Quality Costs in R and D", *10th Annual Western Regional Conference*, ASQC, Feb 63

Roth, H. P. and Morse W.J., "Let's Help Measure and Report Quality Costs", *Management Accounting*, August 1983, pp. 50-53

Rydeski, J. A., "Expose Losses With Quality Costs" *Quality*, May 78, pp. 32-33

Scanlon, F., "Cost Reduction Through Quality Management", *34th ATC*, Atlanta, May 80

Scanlon, F., "Cost Improvement Through Quality Improvement", *35th AQC*, 1981

Scanlon, F., "Management of Quality in a Non-Manufacturing Environment" *37th AQC*, Boston, May 83

Schafer, R. E., "Bayasian Operating Characteristic and Quality", *Industrial Quality Control*, Sep 64

Schecter, E. W., "Better Products at Lower Costs", FAM

Schin, R., "Can Quality Control Pay its Own Way?", *11th Annual Metropolitan Section Conference*, Sep 59

Schliecher, W. F., "Quality Control Circles Save Lockheed Nearly $3 Million", *Quality*, May 77, pp. 14-17

Schmidt, J.W.; Taylor, R.E., "Measuring the Cost of Product Quality" *Society of Automotive Engineers*, vol. 90, no. 6 1982

Schmidt, J. W.,; Taylor, R. E., "A Dual Purpose Cost Based Quality Control System" *Technometrics* 15, 1973, p. 151

Schuck H. E., "Societal and Regulatory Costs", *34th ATC*, Atlanta, May 1980

Schuler, W., "Multistage Sampling Procedures Based on Prior Distributions and Costs", *Annual Mathematical Statistics Journal* 33, 1967, pp. 464-470

Scott, D. C., "Quality Must be Expressed in Terms of Earnings, Costs, Profits, and Customer Satisfaction", *Quality Assurance*, FAM

Seder, L. A., "How to Evaluate a Company's Quality Control Need", *1961 ATC*, pp. 1-8

Sesson, L. "The Life Cycle Cost Procurement Model", *Quality*, Oct 75, pp. 9-11

Shahnazarian, T. E., "Practical Aids, Gaging Cost Analysis", *Industrial Quality Control*, Vol 18, no 12, 1962, pp. 36-40

Shahnazarian, T. E., "Selection of Economical Quality Levels for Multicomponent Assemblies", *Industrial Quality Control*, Oct 65

Shainin, D.; Krensky, P. D.; Dawes, E. W., "Can Quality Cost Principles be Applied to Product Liability?" *33rd ATC*, 1979, pp. 295-296

Shue, E. L.; Jones, H. L., "Higher Quality at Lower Costs", *Factory*, May 67, pp. 86-88

Siff, W. C., "Controlling Quality in a Plastics Processing Plant", *17th Annual Technical Conference*, Society of Plastics Engineers, Jan 61

Siff, W., "Quality Costs in the Process Industries", *37th AQC*, Boston, May 83

Sink, S., "Using Quality Costs in Productivity Measurement" *37th AQC*, Boston, May 83

Sittig, J., "The Economic Choice of Sampling Systems in Acceptance Sampling", *Bulletin of International Statistics Institute* 33, 1951, pp. 51-84

Smith, B. E., "Economics of Sampling Inspection", *Industrial Quality Control*, Mar 65

Squires, F.H., "Quality Control from Bench to Budget", *11th ATC*, Detroit, 1957

Stalcup, R. W., "Our Only Output is Information", *35th AQC*

Stenecker, R. G., "Attacking Quality Costs", *28th ATC*, May 74, pp. 2-1-207

Stephen, F. F., "Monetary Evaluation of Samples in Auditing and Inspection", *15th Annual Metropolitan Section Conference*, Spe 63

Steward, R. H., "Flexible Budgets — The Soundest Way of Controlling QC Costs", *1955 ATC*, New York, pp. 282-290

Stiles, E. M., *Handbook for Total Quality Assurance*, Complete Management Library Vol XXVI, Prentice Hall, 1978, pp. 89-96

Straley, R. L., "Lower Costs Through Total Reliability", *21st ATC*, Chicago, May 67

Stransky, C. C. "Government Quality Assurance Costs", *22nd ATC* May 68

Sullivan, E., "Quality Costs", *Quality Progress*, Apr 83, pp. 24-25

Sullivan, E. and Owens, D.A., "Catching a Glimpse of Quality Costs Today", *Quality Progress*, Dec 83, pp. 21-24

Swift, W. E., "Cost Optimized Calibration", *Quality*, Feb 79, pp. 22-24

Szymanski, E. T., "Relationship of Financial Information and Quality Costs", *39th AQC*, May 1985

Szymanski, E. T., "Overcoming Regulatory Constraints in Quality Costs", *36th AQC*, May 82

Taylor, H. M., "The Economic Design of Cumulative Sum Control Charts", *Technometrics* 10, 1963, pp. 479-488

Thoday, W.R.B., "The Equation of Quality and Profit", *Quality Assurance*, Jun 76, pp. 48-52

Timblin, S. W., "Implementation of Specific Quality Cost Improvement Programs, *22nd ATC*, May 69

Traver, R. W., "Reducing Total Quality Costs", *Automation*, Feb 71

Triplett, W. A., "Support System Cost Effectiveness", *23rd ATC*, May 69

Bibliography

Whitton, A. W., "Methods for Selling Total Quality Control Cost Systems", *26th ATC*, May 72

Wilhelm, W.C., "Quality Program Modeling for Cost Effective Tailoring", *34th ATC*, 1982

Willhite, K.R., "How to Get the Most Out of a QC Budget", *10th ATC*, Montreal, 1956, pp. 651-662

Williams, R.J., "Guide for Reducing Quality Costs", *36th AQC*, May 82

Williams, H.D., "Quality Plus Productivity Plus Cost Equals Profit", *Quality Progress*, Oct 84

Winchell, W. O., "The Hidden Aspect of Vendor Quality Costs", *Akron-Canton Fall Workshop*, Nov 5, 76

Winchell, W. O., "Guide for Managing Vendor Quality Costs", *35th AQC*, 1981

Winchell, W., "Reducing Failure Costs and Measuring Improvement" *37th AQC*, Boston, May 83

Wortham, A. W., "Management Development through Quality Control", *Industrial Quality Control*, Jun 61, pp. 5-7

Wright, C., "Quality Costs: The Effective Measurement of Progress", *Quality Assurance*, May 81, San Francisco

Zabecki, D. T., "Contribution Margin Analysis of Quality Costs", *Quality Progress*, Oct 77, pp. 34-36

Zaludova, A. H., "Quality Optimization Via Total Quality Costs", *35th AQC*, 1981

Zeller, H.J., "Strategic Planning of Quality and Its Assurance", *35th ATC*, May 81, San Francisco

Zerfas, J.F., "Guide for Reducing Quality Costs", *34th ATC*, Atlanta, May 80